CISTERCIAN FATHERS SERIES : NUMBER THIRTY-NINE

JOHN OF FORD

SERMONS ON THE SONG OF SONGS, II

JOHN of FORD

Volume Two
(SERMONS 15–28)

Translated by
WENDY MARY BECKETT

CISTERCIAN FATHERS SERIES : NUMBER THIRTY-NINE

SERMONS ON THE FINAL VERSES OF THE SONG OF SONGS

CISTERCIAN PUBLICATIONS: *Kalamazoo, Michigan 1982*

The editors wish to express their appreciation to Mr John Nixon for his help in preparing the manuscript for publication

This translation is based on the critical Latin edition of the sermons prepared by Edmund Mikkers and Hilary Costello and published in the series CORPUS CHRISTIANORUM, *Continuatio Mediaevalis* XVII & XVIII.

Latin title: *Ioannis de Forda, Super extremam partem cantici canticorum sermones cxx.*

Available in Great Britain and Europe through
A. R. Mowbray & Co. Ltd St Thomas House
Becket Street, Oxford OX1 1SJ

Library of Congress Cataloguing in Publication Data (Revised)

John, Abbot of Ford.
Sermons on the final verses of the Song of Songs.
(Cistercian Fathers series ; no. 29, 39)
Translation of Ioannis de Forda Super extremam partem Cantici canticorum sermones CXX.
On Spine: on the Song of Songs.
Includes bibliographical references.
CONTENTS: 1. Sermons 1-14–2. Sermons 15-28
1. Bible. O.T. Song of Solomon–Sermon s

1. Bible. O.T. Song of Solomon–Sermons.
2. Catholic Church–Sermons. 3. Sermons, English–Translations from Latin. 4. Sermons, Latin–Translations into English. I. Title.
II. Title: On the Song of Songs.
BS1485.J6413 223'.907 77-3697
ISBN 0-87907-629-1 (v. 1) AACR1

Book design by Gale Akins.
Printed in the United States of America.

TABLE OF CONTENTS

SERMONS

SERMONS ON THE SONG OF SONGS, II

SERMON FIFTEEN

The beginning of the fifteenth sermon. How hair, curls and locks, all mean the same, but the implications differ. Why it was that the Nazarenes so carefully cherished the hair of their heads. Who the woman was who shaved the head of Samson while he slept. How the words of the bride in praise of the hair of Jesus fits in with the praise John utters when it is compared to pure wool.

'HIS LOCKS are graceful as the palm-tree, black as the raven.'* Praise of the spouse's locks follows naturally enough upon praise of his head. Locks do not only fit closely with the head but grow from it, and after praise for the head, they come first in the enumeration of his beauties. Yet, if you look at the external form of this description, the words of praise have no praise in them at all, they are almost a criticism, in not hesitating to compare the most beautiful among the sons of men* to the blackness of a raven.

Sg 5:11

Ps 45:2

But to anyone of you going into the wedding feast and approaching the wedding song, I say, Go in, blessed of the Lord; Why wait outside? The secrets of the bed chamber are profound and inaccessible, and the mysteries of the royal bower being sweeter are likewise even more secret. The door is open only to

friends. It is the glory of God to conceal his
Pr 25:2 word,* and he utters it only to those whom he loves and who love him. Speaking of his soul's beloved, the Father says that 'his voice
Is 42:2 will not be heard in the streets'.* 'In the streets', then, as has been said elsewhere, in the streets are the dogs, in the streets are the resentful and quarrelsome, in the streets are those who envy their brother's salvation, who refuse to go in when the Father asks. In the streets also are those who have with them no oil so as to be able to enter the wedding
Cf. Mt 25:11 feast,* and, in short, all those who know nothing of the joy of the marriage and abandon themselves completely, shameful though it is, to whatever belongs 'in the streets'. But as far as we are concerned, if we go humbly to the door of the bed chamber and knock with loving confidence, I am quite certain that the doorkeeper, because he is full of loving-kindness and knows each of us by
Cf. Lk 12:36 name, will open to us.*

2. Now, if you please, let us compare this praise of the locks of the spouse and that tribute to his hair, which in the Book of Revelation John says he saw. 'His hair,' he
Rv 1:14 says, 'is like white wool, white as snow.'* If these two sentences are compared together, as far as appearances go, they are superficially in flat contradiction. Strong, lofty trees are compared with pure wool, and the blackness of the raven to the whiteness of snow. So in the literal, surface sense outside the gates, as it were, there is conflict, but after entry into the marriage chamber where wisdom arranges all things graciously, there is no discord;

supreme agreement.

First it must be observed that hair, curls, and locks all refer to the same thing because they all refer to the hair of the head, but the implications of the terms differ. Hair, irrespective of how it is arranged on the head, applies to the whole and to each separate hair. Hair that has been rolled becomingly into ringlets is called curls. Finally, hair neatly combed and arranged with unpretentious care is known as locks. When the spouse praised the bride, it was not just by chance that he commended her hair first, and then her curls as well. There was a deliberate implication here, that progress in love means growth in beauty and is an incentive to the love and praise of the spouse. His words are: 'You have wounded my heart, my sister, my bride, you have wounded my heart with one glance of your eyes, with one curl of your neck.'* To this twofold praise with which the *Sg 4:9*
spouse greeted her, the bride on this occasion responded in simple terms by praising his hair in the way we have seen. But following from this, I find the spouse paying joint tribute to the hair of the bride's head and to the head itself. 'Your head,' he says, 'is as Carmel, and hair of your head like purple, holding kings captive in its tresses.'* *Sg 7:5*

3. To say something first about hair: when the Lord Jesus was preaching to his disciples about the constancy of the martyr, preparing the mountains with his strength, girded with might,* we find him speaking like *Ps 65:6*
this: 'The hairs of your head are all numbered.'* And again: 'Not a hair of your head *Lk 12:7*

Lk 21:18 will perish.'* So great was the power of what
he said that they took new strength from this
Cf. Ps 33:6 word from heaven,* especially when the Spir-
it, the Paraclete, was sent by the Father in the
name of Jesus to bring to their minds these
Cf. Jn 14:26 and other things he had said to them.* The
hairs growing from the heads of the martyrs,
therefore, are the thoughts and desires of
their hearts, firmly rooted in the charity of
Cf. Eph 3:17 Christ,* and assembling in their countless
numbers against all the strength of this world,
Cf. Rv 7:9 like the power of a vast army.*

Hairs such as these can be cut with the
blade and show neither wound nor bruise, yet
by enduring with a kind of imperturbable
courage, they beautify and strengthen the
heart. In the minds of the brave, how greatly
these thoughts increase in depth and number
when the blast of persecution threatens, when
God stirs up the deeps of the sea, the roaring
Ps 65:7 of its waves!* Is not Jesus aroused, who
previously happened to be asleep? Is it not
then that the arrows of prayer take on a keen-
er edge, and the fire of meditation flares up?
Is this not the time when the exhortations of
the evangelists and the prophets are more
frequently recalled, and the eternal judge-
ments of God thoughtfully remembered?
Surely it is now that the finest examples of
the virtues come to mind, and, what streng-
thens the heart more than all else, the
memory of Our Lord's passion and the
weight of glory that will come upon us, a
weight which the passing sufferings of this
present time render measurelessly immense
Cf. Rm 8:18 in its sublimity.*

Without any doubt at all, hairs of this kind do not take their origin just from the mind of the martyrs, but from their head, which is Christ. This is borne out by the words: 'We are not sufficient to think anything of ourselves, as from ourselves, but our sufficiency is from God.'* And so they are numbered by him who gave them, and they do not perish, because they are protected by him now and will be rewarded by him in the end. Anyone who is well-endowed with this kind of hair may well boast and say: 'We have more on our side than they have'.* And so much for their abundance.

2 Co 3:5

2 K 6:16

4. As for their strength, should he not sing out with joy: 'Though an army should stand against me, my heart will not fear.'* Yet in the wonderful strength of these hairs there is one very great danger, that someone take pride in them as if they drew their root from somewhere else than from him of whom it is said: 'The head of the man is Christ.'* It is of Christ that the martyrs raise the loud cry: 'The Lord of hosts is with us, the God of Jacob is our stronghold.'*

Ps 27:3

1 Co 11:3

Ps 46:7

5. If you find yourself in possession of this blessing, be very careful to cling to him who is your head and to adorn this head. Take thought only for his glory, and you in your turn will receive glory from him. Remember, turn it over in your mind, that it is he who creates these hairs whose strength is so great, he who counts them, he who washes them, he who arranges and tends them. He creates them by the promptings of the Holy Spirit, he counts them by increasing

them through grace, he washes them through the sanctifying power of compunction, he arranges them by the restraints of prudence, he tends them by the gracious gift of humility. Fix your thoughts on the loving-kindness of the creator, the generosity of the giver, the tenderness of the sanctifier, the watchful care of the ruler, and finally, the providence of the guardian who keeps you safe. When hair is like this, so cared for and seemly, you need not fear to describe it as locks, perfectly in keeping with the head of the spouse.

Yet, oh, how tepid we are! How careless we are of our thoughts! We find ourselves so wasteful of our heart, though we have been warned to protect it with every safeguard.* We are so sluggish to do ourselves good, so prompt to do ourselves harm. Since we have a firm promise, from the very mouth of truth itself, that all the hairs of our head have been counted,* that every good and holy thought has a claim to share one day in the eternal blessedness of his glory, why do we not press on with the utmost energy to multiply these thoughts? Why do we let any hour escape us?* Why let even a moment slip past? Although it has a special significance for them, it was not only to the martyrs that the promise was made that: 'their reward is with the Lord, and their thought with the Most High.'* By cleaving most firmly to their head, they have attained an invincible strength beyond that of others, and neither things present nor things to come nor any creature whatever* is able to tear them away from their head, however varied or searching their torments.

Cf. Pr 4:23

Lk 12:7

Cf. Persius, Satirae *5:153.*

Ws 5:16

Cf. Rm 8:38, 1 Co 3:22.

6. Yet, sad though it is, there were not a few whose hair fell away and who were not strong enough to answer the question of their torturers. Why do you think this should have happened to them, if not because they presumed too much on themselves and too little on their head? It is an inalterable rule that whoever makes flesh his arm* is a man of flesh, and if he has prepared horses for the day of battle, they are found on that day to be flesh and not spirit.* As an example for us, there is that great champion of the Lord, Samson, the strongest of men.* We read that he was the Lord's Nazarene, privileged with strength above all normal human standards, and his strength resided in the hair of his head. How did it come about that this hero withered away so pitifully, without battle, untouched by blow or violence? To his shame, all his strength suddenly fell into ruin in the lap of a wanton woman, and while he slept it was quietly stolen away. In your opinion, who is this woman who furtively undermines the brave, who counterfeits love and, then, while they sleep, stays awake herself to do them harm, working mischief like a sharpened razor?* I consider this woman the inordinate desire for vainglory, all gentle woman in bearing and manner, and proportionately strong in seducing and betrayal. How often, to our grief, this woman wreaks great havoc among brave men in this mortal world! How often she has applied her razor to consecrated hair, how many heads she has shaved, how many eyes she has blinded!

Cf. Jr 17:5

Cf. Is 31:3

Cf. Jg 16

Cf. Ps 52:2

Notice, first, how Samson is battered by

the woman with question after question. Only at the very end does he reveal to her that all his strength lies in his hair. There are those who bless brave men to their faces, who extoll their heroic deeds, who praise and glorify them. Under the guise of admiration, is not this subtly to put the question which the Jews raised about the Lord: 'Where did this
Mt 13:54 wisdom and these mighty deeds come from?'* This is how they strive to beguile our Samson with their razor, saying with treacherous flattery: 'What have you to do with us, Jesus,
Mt 8:29 Son of God?* We know who you are, God's
Mk 1:24 holy one.'* But our Samson showed for the future how this temptation is to be resisted: 'he rebuked them, and would not allow them
Lk 4:41 to speak.'* So if the throat of this woman is smoother than oil, in the end it is sharp as a
Cf. Pr 5:4 two-edged sword and bitter as gall.* She comes in gently, but at the last bites like a
Pr 23:32 serpent and stings like an adder.* Therefore, you who are brave men—if you are genuinely brave—be on your guard not to grow weak under this questioning. Whatever that woman says to your face is a conspiracy against
Cf. Is 8:12 you.* In her mouth she has a blessing, but in her heart a curse, in her home a razor, and at her back the Philistines. Rebuke instantly, rebuke vigorously, do not even let them speak, those whose praises are a plot against you, those who extoll you only to deceive, and laud you to the skies only to cast you down.

7. If you have noticed, then, what is really denoted by these hairs of his (Samson), I think you will grasp why the bride compares

the locks of the spouse to palm trees. For the palm, in a figurative but commonly-accepted sense, is said to represent victory, and it is given to those who conquer in the struggle as a manifest mark of final victory. This is why the Apocalypse tells us that 'those who come out of great tribulation and have washed their robes in the blood of the lamb',* are said *Rv 7:14*
to have palms in their hands.* What else can *Cf. Rv 7:9*
this signify but the virtue of patience, through which they joyfully triumphed in this life, or else the reward of patience, by which they were established still more joyfully in the glory of the life to come? Indeed, this patience reigned supreme in the midst of their enemies; in the midst of their combats it went on its way, rejoicing like a conqueror, carrying about with it the banners of its glory. It was radiant in its trust, it exulted in its trials, it gave thanks to God for all these things.* Like the palm, the more laden it is, *Cf. Ph 3:7*
the more it flourishes, and the more densely it is pressed about, the more boldly it lifts itself up on high. Surely this virtue is well named, 'the palm' or 'victory', because it conquers by the very means by which it seems conquered or conquerable! Whatever the world thinks will damage it, it turns to gain. It draws help from tribulation, changes sorrow into joy, turns abundance of grief into a wealth of consolation.* *Cf. Jn 16:20*

Our first martyr has an apt name, Stephen, which means 'crowned', for he was not only to be crowned in his glorification, but he was also crowned here [on earth] in his patience. This is why the martyrs sing on their lyres:

'Lord, you have crowned us with your favor
Ps 5:12 as with a shield.'* 'Lord, in your strength the
king will rejoice, and in your salvation he will
Ps 21:1 greatly exult.'* And again: 'We will not fear,
Ps 46:2 though the earth should rock,'* because 'the
Ps 46:7 Lord of hosts is with us.'* Because of the
Lord, even 'the streams of the river make
Ps 46:4 glad the city of God.'* Not to mention that
exultant cry: 'My ears will hear the doom of
my evil assailants; the just man will flourish
Ps 92:11-12 like the palm tree.'*

See how the just boast of being crowned by
the Lord while the impious weave them a
crown of thorns; for in the power of God,
which is the suffering of Christ, they are con-
fident of reigning with him as kings. And
since in the hope of eternal joy and the joy
of that hope amidst their afflictions, they
receive in advance the pledge of eternal life,
they reckon (their sufferings) as no more than
a little trinket given them by the Holy Spirit,
for the just man will flourish like the palm
Ps 92:12 tree.*

But we must realize that the patience of the
just is not always made glad uninterruptedly.
It does not fall to everyone to say with Paul:
Rm 5:3 'More than that, we rejoice in our sufferings.*
A claim such as his is, indeed, the right of
towering and lofty palms which have ad-
vanced gradually to their degree of height
and glory, according as they were blessed by
God, whose law controls them. So they go
Ps 84:7 from strength to strength,* and they grow
from palm trees into lofty and graceful
palms. It is a great thing indeed to have borne
in the hand a branch from a tree like this, and

to go forward with it to meet the Lord Jesus. It is a greater thing faithfully to have planted in the courts of God some shoot of this tree. It is greater still to behold the palm actually growing there. Yet by far the greatest joy comes from seeing it bear fruit and being able to say: 'I will go up to the palm tree and take hold of its fruit.'* *Sg 7:8*

Hence the man who cuts off a palm branch for himself is one who, without having put on enough of the virtue of patience to withstand everything, especially the injuries inflicted by others, nevertheless tempers with the gentleness of long suffering bodily discomforts and the trials of illness and adversity. He will take the cup without complaint, as if it were offered by the Lord's hand, and he will say: 'I will receive the cup of salvation and call upon the name of the Lord.'* *Ps 116:13*

8. There are others, not satisfied with this amount of patience, who intend to bear patiently all troubles, from whatever source. They are fully confident that there is no disaster in the city which is not the Lord's doing,* and in no way shuffle the blame on to their neighbor. They know it is Jesus who draws the sea together, and likewise they know it is Jesus, too, who gives the sea orders, he who divided the waters when and how he pleased, and yet it is also he who walks upon its waves.* They believe that nothing is done by Jesus that is not in accordance with his name, nothing that is not loving and for our our good, and in this confidence they send down ever deeper the roots of their intention. They become planted in the house of

Cf. Am 3:6

Cf. Mt 14:25

Ps 92:13 the Lord* and planted together with Christ in
Rm 6:5 the likeness of his death.* It follows naturally
that they should blossom in the hope of
eternal glory, while patience itself turns sweet,
and, it is written, 'A cheerful heart produces a
Pr 17:22 blooming life.'* But flowers lead to fruit,
for the hope of happiness matures into a kind
of happiness in hope, and to pluck the [fruit
and have a] foretaste of eternal joy is not
without an immense joy of its own.

Men of this type know by experience what
the firstfruits of the spirit are like, they have
savored the fruits of the spiritual palm, which
the apostle calls 'justice and peace and joy in
Rm 14:17 the Holy Spirit'.* Such a man really towers,
not one of a grove of low and stunted trees,
Cf. Si 24:18 (Vulg.) but exalted like a plam tree in Kadesh,* so
that he may glory with them and say: 'What is
Rm 5:3 more, we glory in our tribulations.'* He does
not say only: 'in the hope of the glory of the
Rm 5:2 sons of God',* as if our joy were merely in
flower, but in our very tribulations themselves we find our glory, regarding them
as fruit which we are already picking.

We have made it quite clear, and indeed it follows of necessity, that the fruit of these tribulations is plentiful and sweet, delightful, giving us health and life. For to begin with, not inconsequential in itself, it forms patience in us, for without trials it would be impossible for us to be taught it. Then, in the second place, through these trials patience becomes the means by which all impurity is refined away from us, as it is tested. Thirdly, once we have been purified by tribulation and our conscience is deeply at peace, we are suddenly renewed. We trustfully raise pure hands and a face shining with oil, and we say: 'You are my patience, Lord;* trusting in you, I shall not fail* and I shall never be put to shame.'* *Ps 71:5* *Ps 26:1* *Ps 31:1*

The way of God's witnesses and martyrs, then, is at first very narrow. Afterwards it becomes very broad and easy, when by means of the palm of patience hope soon springs up from tribulation. Patience goes ahead of charity to prepare the way, so that when she begins her journey, she may quickly set her feet on the path and rejoice like a giant to run her course.* *Ps 19:5*

9. These towering trees have only one thing to fear, but it is a great fear. It is possible that they may glory in their preeminence, may marvel at their own loftiness, may, because of their height, be heedless of the Most High, who is in the heavens. It is possible that sometime one of them may say to himself: 'I consider myself to have won already.'* The judgment of the watchmen is to be feared lest some terrible verdict be pronounced against them. Some day the Holy One, the watchman of heaven, will cry out: 'Cut down the tree, tear off its branches, scatter its fruit.'* That heavenly condemnation is the only thing that the graceful palm must hold in dread. *Cf. Ph 3:13* *Dn 4:11*

Graceful and high, the palm has only one support to hold it firm: that it be as lowly as it is lofty. It is great in everything, and in the same proportion, it must humble itself in everything. If its humility does not match its height, the beauty of its holiness will be

something less than perfect, the two virtues will not balance each other. To keep its graceful elevation free from blemish, to save it from the least touch of vanity, let the palm become black and in its bearing like the raven. I will speak more plainly: let them be high, not think lofty thoughts, but humble and sharing the thoughts of the humble. Let them ascend to the heavens; but so as not to fall like any of
Cf. Ps 82:7 the princes,* let them descend with care to the depths. Let them be successful in imitating Paul and following him when he leaves his mind for the sake of God; but likewise let them accompany him when he returns to us, made sober once more for our sake. In other words, in the very midst of these wonderful exultations of theirs, let them always remember the contemptible sight of their face in its native blackness. Let the downfall of eminent men be fixed before their eyes in season and out of season and let their countenance reflect always the aspect of the judgment of God.

10. From what has been said, I think it is very evident how the vision of John, far from contradicting the words of the bride, are in full conformity with them. In comparing the hair of the Son of man to pure wool, he obviously means to imply the holy gentleness of patience, shining forth in the sublime majesty of the saint of saints. The meekness of patience, which contains within itself the radiance of humility, is likewise indicated by adding a comparison with snow. These are the two virtues, as if they were identical twins hand in hand, that the Lord himself places before us as what we

must see and imitate in him. 'Learn of me,' he says, 'for I am meek and humble of heart, and you will find rest for your souls.'* *Mt 11:29*
Otherwise there will be no rest, but deep unrest and an unbreachable split in the body of the virtues, if submission lacks the weight of humility or humility is without the gentleness of submission. So in all that pertains to the essence of virtue, the blackness of a raven in one place and the whiteness of snow in another place mean exactly the same, or they differ only very slightly. The blackness of the raven is an instinctive abasement, showing a man to himself and to the world as contemptible. On the other hand, the whiteness of snow is a lowly disposition of the heart, showing the heart what it is and pleasing the divine majesty by its spontaneous subjection. So the blackness gives shape to the whiteness, while the whiteness infuses the blackness with gentle charm. Blackness humiliates the outer man and binds the inner man captive; but whiteness renews the inner man and heals the outer, so that the heart, influenced by both colors—white and black—is able to say: 'I am black but beautiful, daughters of Jerusalem.'* *Sg 1:4*

But now the scope of this sermon is insistently demanding a conclusion, one which we desire and seek, namely, that we too may deserve to be found among those hairs which are all counted and of which not one will be lost.* *Cf. Mt 10:30*
And of this we have assurance through our head, the Only-begotten Son of God the Father who with the same Father and the Holy Spirit lives and reigns, God for ever and ever. Amen.

SERMON SIXTEEN

The beginning of the sixteenth sermon. How the eyes of the spouse means those who have deserved to enjoy the sight of the Word Incarnate. Why these eyes are called doves, by the bride or by Isaiah or by the Lord himself. Why they are compared at one time to clouds and at another to serpents.

'HIS EYES are doves beside springs of water, bathed in milk, at rest near full
Sg 5:12 flowing streams.'* After praise of his head and his locks, the beloved lifts up her eyes to the eyes of her beloved. It is clear that gazing at them held her absorbed for rather a long time, because in praising them she does not use at all the same brevity which sufficed before. When the bride surveys the whole loveliness of her spouse, his eyes allure and speak to her of his love, and this causes some delay. On his eyes her gaze dwells more fixedly, she praises them at greater length and fulness, she surrounds and caresses them with finer eloquence. It cannot be overlooked that the eyes hold a position of undisguised prominence, and that they have been allotted a place of great glory in the countenance of glory. It is these eyes that themselves announce their glory when they say: 'We have seen his glory, the glory as of the only-

begotten of the Father.'* I take this as referring quite obviously to the eyes of the spouse, because the apostle testifies: 'No one knows the things of a man except the spirit of a man that is in him, so no one knows the things of God except the Spirit of God.'* And to prove this, the apostle calls Isaiah to witness: 'Eye has not seen, O God, what things you have prepared for those who love you.'* So those who saw the glory of Jesus were really the eyes of Jesus.

Jn 1:14

1 Co 2:11

Is 64:3, Cf. 1 Co 2:9

2. Blessed indeed were those eyes—we have it on the word of the very one who pronounced a blessing on them in glory—who saw what they saw!* They saw the only-begotten in the bosom of the Father,* they saw him whom the angels long to look upon,* they were considered worthy, not once or twice or three times, but daily and almost continually to behold, to regard, to observe, and most deeply to contemplate him, and by the constant sight of that lovely and compelling countenance to fan for themselves the torch of sweetest love, and to seal on that image of the living God within them the loving imprint of the light of God's own face. Yet this kind of sight was still corporeal to some extent. They were not yet able to exult and cry: 'Even though we once knew Christ in the flesh, yet we do so now no longer.'* It was a glory surpassing all the glory of this world, a happiness richer than all the pleasures of the body, to cleave to the Word appearing in the flesh, to speak with him, to share his home, to live his life, to have seen God in human flesh, not now through a mirror and dimly,

Cf. Lk 10:23

Jn 1:18

1 Pt 1:12

2 Cor 5:7

1 Co 13:12 but face to face.'*

The prophets and the just who lived before the coming of Christ are considered holy because they longed to behold this sight. Abraham saw him for a moment in the spirit *Cf. Jn 8:56* and was filled with joy,* through his ineffable happiness keeping that one fleeting glimpse as a day of uninterrupted festival. If this is so, what a festival this sight must have been in the hearts of those who loved him, revealing to their blessed eyes the son of the virgin, the king of the angels, the Lord of all creation, and revealing all this shining forth in this man! Since the invisible things of God are clearly seen through those that have *Rm 1:20* been made,* how blessed is the philosophy of these sages! To behold the majesty of God, the wisdom of God, the goodness of God, they had no need of relying on many steps or immersing themselves in the complications of disputed points. They had simply to return the gaze of their beloved, standing behind our *Cf. Sg 2:9* wall, and gazing on us through the window* of our senses. Only the thickness of one wall, only one step, separated them from the ineffable contemplation of the eternal light which is in heaven! One of them, indeed, the very last, was healed and saved by one long look from Jesus, and the profit of that momentary vision wiped out the debts of all the years. He quickly caught up with the *Cf. Lk 19* apostles who had gone before.* Indeed, with other disciples, too, the wisdom of God could have spared them all labors of their own and with the same ease have brought them swiftly to perfection.

3. But, because of his indescribable kindness, which made him appear on the earth and live among men, the Wisdom of God consented to assume the appearance of toil in the giving of a command and first anointed the eyes of the blind with the clay of his flesh and then ordered light to shine from the darkness; next by degrees he produced from these eyes stars and then, after the stars, created the sun and its rising. So those eyes shone as if fixed in the sky, which is the face of Jesus, and as if they were the noonday sun, and they gave light to the earth. Through them, just as through his own eyes, the Lord looked down from heaven on all who dwell on the earth,* taking away the darkness of ungodliness, drying up the clay of wickedness, and through them making known to the world the paths of life. *Ps 33:13*

All these stars I would describe as a single sun, because in what pertains to the unity of doctrine, one plants and another waters, but they are one.* On the other hand, as regards charity, in both kinds of love they are fiery, or rather in flame. In Daniel, the eyes of the son of man are compared to flames of fire.* In the psalm, the ministers of our God are described as a flaming fire.* *1 Co 3:8* *Cf. Rv 1:14* *Cf. Ps 104:4*

4. And so, these eyes of the spouse, burning like the sun with a twofold flame of charity, suffered violent constraint as to which love they should more especially abandon themselves. For to be dissolved and to be with Christ was their supreme desire, but the other charity, though less in its affective power but more irresistible in its strength compelled

them to think of their little ones and to bide with them until they were weaned. Their love for God was sweeter, but the love for his sons was more pressing. The one was more peaceful, the other more insistent. And indeed this love towards one's neighbor is of a lesser kind, but in the dispensation of the wisdom of God, disposing all within his house wisely and sweetly, there was a tranquil readiness for the greater to yield and become the servant of the less.

In that love which is directed towards God they alone know what fervor and light they drew from the blessed sight of Jesus before his passion and after his glorious resurrection. Theirs was a secret and a love shared between themselves and their beloved, the head. However in their love for God's sons countless and evident signs gave evidence of its tenderness, sweetness and amplitude. If the tenderness of the love is in question, hear what one of them said on behalf of all: 'Who is weak, and I am not weak? Who is scandalized, and I am not
2 Cor 11:29 on fire?'* If the sweetness is, listen to the
following: 'I take God for my witness, that I
yearn after all of you with the affection of
Ph 1:8 Christ Jesus.'* And again: 'So, my brothers,
whom I love and long for, my joy and my
Ph 4:1 crown, so stand fast in the Lord, my beloved.'*
And regarding the greatness of this love: 'I
will most gladly spend and be spent for your
2 Co 12:15 souls.'* Eyes like this are surely not so much
flaming, but, as it is written of them, 'a flame
Cf. Rv 1:14 of fire'!* Surely they are not so much dove-
like as actually doves, and moreover, doves
Sg 5:12 bathed in milk!*

5. 'His eyes,' she says, 'are doves beside springs of water, bathed in milk.' 'Doves' is well chosen, for they are artless in their innocence, swift in flight, united in love, fruitful in offspring, tender in sighing. So too, they were innocent in bearing injuries without retaliation, swift in bestowing a kindness, eager in reviving and preserving charity, zealous in bringing to life the little buds of an ever-growing piety devoted to maturing and forming them. It is specially in their regard that the prophets and the evangelists say: 'Who are these that fly like a cloud and like doves to their windows?'* And again: 'Be wise as serpents and simple as doves.'* How bewildering, how wonderful, these words from so many ages before, greeting from afar those men of virtue, who are those 'who fly like a cloud and like doves to their windows!'*

Is 60:8
Mt 10:16
Is 60:8

6. This double flight, what is its purpose in these great friends of God? They fly for our sake, they fly back for their own sake. They fly like clouds to make us fruitful, they fly back to their windows to ponder themselves. Externally they are usefully at work; internally they are humbly at rest. They offer to the external view what they have internally arranged should be shown forth; they subject to a close internal scrutiny whatever they have revealed externally, analyzing its goodness or badness. In a real sense, they are clouds raining down to us the just one, so that the earth, drenched with them, may open and bud forth a savior.* As they freely received the rain coming down to them from above, so they freely poured it back to us down below.

Is 45:8

For rain is certainly free, coming down from the pure and most loving will of him who is the Father of rain, and through the willing service of these men he sends it out to purify and make fruitful the will of men. 'In this service they attribute nothing to themselves'. In this service they claim no credit for themselves but rather for God who gives the rain and the increase; they await only the eternal reward of their toil. And then they are doves at their windows, when in all simplicity they preach to us the word of life, not seeking our possessions but ourselves.

From those clouds there sometimes issued the thunder of some sharp rebuke or the lightning flash revealing some terrible misdeed or refuting some error or impiety; but the wonderful gentleness and piety from which such awesome manifestations sprang was shown by the generous downpour of consolation which immediately followed, turning all the previous thunder and lightning
Cf. Ps 135:7 into rain.* 'For I wrote to you,' said one of them, 'out of much affliction and anguish of heart and with many tears, not to cause you pain, but to let you know how dear you were
2 Co 2:4 to me.'* And again: 'Although I made you sad by my letter, I do not regret it; and yet I did regret it, for I see that letter grieved you, though only for a while. As it is I rejoice, not because you grieved, but because you were
2 Co 7:8-9 grieved into repenting.'* We may see thunder and lightning in the clouds, but we will also see St Paul like a dove tenderly murmuring and sweetly sighing. So in these doves there is much simplicity yet great authority and

plentiful wisdom. 'Be wise as serpents,' said the Lord, 'and simple as doves.'* *Mt 10:16*

7. There is indeed much wisdom in the serpent, but its purpose is to deceive and destroy. It comes gliding along, creeping secretly, slithering furtively forward to make a sudden attack. Then in one fleeting prick of a minute fang, it pours deadly poison into the whole body. That serpent is visible, but there is also an invisible one, lying in ambush for our heel.

Yet be aware, we are given a completely new kind of serpent! These are serpents strong with a greater wisdom, who lift up a sign for us in the midst of the nation,* serpents who teach us to fix our gaze on the bronze serpent.* One look at him is antidote enough for the snake's poison, because he is himself so untouched by snake's poison. These serpents wind their gracious way into the human heart. It is not on the seductive words of human wisdom they rely, as if walking in human fashion, but rather they came breathing out the doctrine of the spirit, almost as if in a gentle hissing sound.* They creep in with much fear and trembling, as though furtively, because they have a real fear that the word of the cross may be foolishness to their listeners.* So they are serpents, opposing the wisdom of God, which the world considers foolishness, to the wisdom of the flesh, and in that wisdom [of God] they are prepared to lift up serpents and lead every mind captive in obedience to Christ.* The serpents of Pharaoh were swallowed up by the serpent of Moses,* for the folly of God is certainly wiser than men.*

Cf. Is 11:12

Cf. Nb 21:8

Cf. 1 Co 1:8

Cf. 2 Co 10:5

Cf. Ex 7:12

1 Co 1:25

This serpentine prudence takes nothing away from the simplicity of the dove, but in the wonderful arrangement of divine wisdom, gives it an edge, while simplicity in turn gently tranquilizes its partner. They were simple as doves who did not adulterate the word of God by a base search for profit, or by intrigue for position and power, or by a hunger for vain glory, or by the leaven of error. Any one of these adulterates the simplicity of a godly sermon and rudely defiles the purity of the Lord's word not only in the mind of the preacher but also in the minds of his hearers. This is the comment of a pure lover of pure speech, a faithful steward: 'We are not, like so many, adulterators of God's
2 Co 2:17 word.* What we preach is not ourselves but Jesus Christ as Lord, with ourselves as
2 Co 4:5 your servants for Jesus' sake.'* And in another place: 'For our appeal does not spring from error or uncleanness, nor is it made with guile . . . for we never used words of flattery, as you know, or a cloak for greed, as God is my witness. We did not seek glory from men, either from you or from others . . . . but we were babes among you, like a nurse taking care of her little ones. So, being affectionately desirous of you, we were ready to share with you not only the gospel of God,
1 Th 2:3-8 but also our own selves.'* Here we have a truly dovelike eye, or, to put it better, a true dove. It looks only at Jesus, with a gaze wholly pure and simple, emulous of his bride in faithful and loving emulation.

Cf. Juvenal, 8. Sad to say, how rare a bird this is in our
Satirae *6.165* land these days!* O church of God, O dove

of Jesus, his pure one, how different are the pastors and teachers you know nowadays! It is a rare one among them who looks deeply at you with the pure gaze of contemplation, whose love, as he runs to your embrace, hastens to your kiss, is not wholly adulterous. For the most part, nearly all of them seek what is theirs, not what is yours; or rather, it is yours they are after, not yourself.* They do not seek your soul, unless it be to take it away. These, too, 'fly like clouds',* towering menacingly above your head, lofty in power, heavy with authority, strong in their splendor. There is certainly the virtue of great splendor in these clouds, but even more certainly this does not come from God. Clouds true enough, but kept aloft by the spirit of this world, swollen with the lust to power, swirling with angry displeasure, tempestuous with strife. Violent threats break from them in savage thunderings, and often they glitter with lightning stabs. Wherever the wind of ambition drives, in whatever direction the hope of worldly gain compels them, there are they borne with frantic haste. No eloquence like dew is to be expected from them,* so that your earth may receive it and give its fruit.* There is no dew of benediction in them, the spirit of God is not on their lips, far less in their hearts.*

Cf. Ph 2:21
Cf. Is 60:8
Cf. Dt 32:2
Cf. Ps 85:12
Cf. Is 29:13

Are you then to think of men such as these as doves rather as ravens or birds of prey? From their fruits, they make themselves known for what they are in their land.* If they were doves, they would meditate like the dove, they would fly like the dove. They

Cf. Mt 12:33

would fly and they would repose; they would fly at times to their own windows, to examine and purify their own conscience. From the the flood of many waters they would fly to the windows of the ark, to the heart of Jerusalem, they would fly to it, not empty-handed, but carrying the fruit of peace and
Cf. Gn 8:11 love.*

As it is, however, their behavior is very different. They are on the watch for blood, their eyes are eager for carrion. Their mouth longs to tear to pieces, there is an evil jubilation in their throat, like one who devours the poor
Hab 3:14 man in secret.* According to that saying of the Lord mentioned before, they are certainly wise as serpents, but they are not simple as
Cf. Mt 10:16 doves.* Like serpents, they sharpen their
Cf. Ps 140:3 tongues* in every kind of quibble, all for the sake of getting hold of and protecting money, and they base their claims on what laws and canons sanction. A two-edged sword is in their hand to wreak vengeance on the na-
Ps 149:6-7 tions,* and they themselves are trained and practised in war, using each hand as a right hand. They are knowing and cunning in the art of justifying the wicked man in exchange for his gifts, and in taking away from the just man his justice. And so they are as wise as serpents, and their motive is to lay a trap for the heel of the simple. All their care goes to protect their own head, to keep the dignity of their position safe from any harm and never to yield any of their glory to someone else. Alas, the venom of adders is on their
Ps 140:3 lips,* and with it they murder not only Eve, but Adam too. With a bile exceedingly bitter,

they devour the people of God like a piece of bread.* Thus with one bite, while they plunder man's bodily substance, they destroy his spiritual wealth which is charity. They do it to death with onslaughts like this.*

Cf. Ps 53:4

Cf. Dt 32:24

Finally, just as is written of the serpent, they are the most cunning of beasts.* They spare their body any labor, they support themselves solely on the pleasurable blossoms of luxury, and they are never without the tenderest of little pillows under each elbow. Every heart alive this day knows suffering, but they are different. All the sons of Adam bear their hereditary load and 'eat their bread in the sweat of their brow,'* but these do not. They slide all work away from their own shoulders and shift it all onto other people, yet every fruit of the work they appropriate to themselves. I pass over in silence whatever lies hidden within, if it can still be spoken of as lying hidden when it is widely known to all and sundry. It is done openly in the full light of day, so their shame can have no concealment and they themselves do not know how to blush. This makes the wounds that these serpents inflict all the more dangerous, for with their bland seductions and vicious example they destroy the very people whom they ought to be healing from the serpent's bite.

Cf. Gn 3:1

Gn 3:19

9. Let no one accuse me of speaking offensively of all those who now bear authority. Even in these days, the Lord has prepared no small lamp for his Christ,* and of that seed which the Lord blessed he has left no small remnant for us.* Let us look, let us

Cf. Ps 132:17

Cf. Is 61:9

rejoice, with great admiration let us cry aloud: 'Who are these who fly like clouds and like doves to their windows?'* There are also those words which the bride said about these men of virtue, when praising her spouse: 'His eyes are doves beside springs of water, bathed in milk, at rest near full flowing streams.'* These men are set high in the sky, through the example of their sublime life, and to all who dwell beneath them they are a shade from the heat by day, and a refuge and a shelter from the storm and the rain.* They do indeed tower aloft like clouds in their splendor and freedom, but very humbly considering themselves lower than others, they fly back to their windows like doves. It may well be that they live in great mansions, but like the dove in the clefts of the rock,* they regard all earthly greatness as cramped and tottering. So like a dove they meditate in the depths of their contemplation; considering all things as transient, thus put no value on them. They long to fly away from the narrow house of their body, as from the small cavern in the rock,* and with inexpressible groaning they yearn after the eternal tabernacles. They say: 'Who will give me wings like a dove, to fly away and be at rest?'* Their eyes turn away from greedy theft as from carrion, and wanting nothing more than unblemished grain, they keep their hands unsoiled by bribery. In their mouth is ever a word of holy encouragement and tender consolation, like some branch of the olive. And so that they may always have something from which to bring forth old and new,* a table is ever spread in their sight,†

Is 60:8

Sg 5:12

Is 4:6

Cf. Sg 2:14

Cf. Sg 2:14

Ps 55:6

**Cf. Mt 13:52.*

and on it are the loaves of proposition. Their haunt is beside springs of water, from which they draw for themselves and also pour out for us, through our Lord, Jesus Christ, only-begotten of the Father, who with the Father and the Holy Spirit lives and reigns God, for ever and ever.
Amen.

SERMON SEVENTEEN

The beginning of the seventeenth sermon. What the rivers are beside which the doves reside. How the spirit represented by the dove hovers over the waters. And how doves, that is, spiritual men, may reside or be borne aloft beside the waters. Of the four kinds of washing with which Jesus washed his disciples, and of the sevenfold spirit he bestowed on them, partly before, partly after his ascension.

'HIS EYES are doves beside springs of water, bathed in milk, at rest near full
Sg 5:12 flowing streams.'* There is something important, something deeply and mysteriously secret that the bride seems to be suggesting to the maidens in this distinction between three different liquids. First she speaks of waters; she calls the second milk; she thinks the third should not be too exactly described. This may be because whatever is meant by 'flowing streams' is something ineffable, or because she wants to give the maidens an occasion to
Cf. Mt 7:7 seek, to ask, to knock;* bread will be more precious to them when they eat it with sweat
Cf. Gn 3:19 on their brow.* She remembers hearing from the wise man: 'Give occasion to a wise man
Pr 9:9 and he will be wiser still.'*

But I could not say to wisdom: 'You are
Pr 7:4 my sister,' nor to call 'prudence my friend'.*

Whenever I have said in my heart: I will seize hold of wisdom and I will become wise, she has gone far away from me, much farther than before. She is deep, profoundly deep, who can find her out?* Yet I recall how it is said of her that 'she speaks to the foolish,'* and that she is under an obligation to the wise and foolish alike.* So we wait, in humility, for her to bless and to break the bread that is set before us. Set before us it whets the appetite, but let it be broken and it satisfies the hungry. The one who sets it out is no other than he who gives food to all living things,* but he is revealed in the blessing of his countenance and he is known in the breaking of bread.*

Qo 7:24-25

Pr 9:4

Cf. Rm 1:14

Ps 136:25

Cf. Lk 24:35

2. The first thing we are told to do, as we take our places at the table of wisdom, is to regard carefully what is being set before us. I understand the doves to be first above springs of water, then washed in milk, and finally resting near full-flowing streams. They are hovering over the first liquid, they are immersed in the second, they are at rest near the third. The first is underneath them, the second above them, the third near them. These are the doves of whom we sing with admiration and delight: 'Who are these who fly like clouds and like doves to their own windows?'* And if we look well at them, we can ponder on three different states in them and, connected with this, three stages of growth in grace, especially after the day of resurrection.

Is 60:8

Their faith in Christ was cruelly wounded by the scandal of the cross, not completely killed, but certainly weakened to the point of death.

Then Christ rose, and little by little their faith began to grow strong again. After forty days it was restored to full health, cured with balm from the healing hand of Jesus. Their hope, too, of which they were so sure, which they rashly promised was of itself strong enough to
Cf. Mt 26:33 remain true to Christ in his passion,* was soon afterwards put to the question by the slightest trial. It tottered and fell and lay helpless, almost at its last breath. Yet at the resurrection of Christ it also was restored to life, and now it realized fully, from its own experience, that the race is not to the swift or the war to the strong, and that it is not in the
Ps 147:10 power of warriors that God takes pleasure.* Men made strong from the day of the resurrection, they began to train for battle, but with a new kind of training where they put their hope not in their bow and their sword. Nor did they lean on that which had struck them, that is to say the staff of their own self confidence. From that day onwards the God of Jacob was to be their rescuer and their hope there was added the gift of knowledge, for Jesus opened their eyes so that they in the power of God through being distrustful of itself. Then to enlighten their faith and their hope there was added the gift of knowledge, for Jesus open their eyes so that they might understand the scriptures. Those eyes, now filled with the light of Jesus, met him on every page and the self assurance of mortal minds was blunted.

3. Furthermore, when Jesus breathes on them, they draw in the spirit of piety for the remission of sins, drawing it from his own

spirit. He himself has said: 'The spirit of the Lord is upon me, because he has anointed me.'* Indeed, the world badly needs a generous outpouring of this upon the disciples. Their hearts should be overflowing with piety which ought to be opened wide to all sinners. These four spirits, then, of faith, fear, knowledge and piety, infused into the lovers of Christ before the solemn and powerful infusion of the spirit, may I not speak of them as 'springs of water'?

Lk 4:18

4. Truly the Holy Spirit was hovering over these waters, and they too with his support and nurture were likewise hovering over them. The Spirit, I repeat, the Holy Spirit is the true dove, the fountainhead of simplicity, charity and innocence, and it is through association with him that those who are worthy of sharing this same name can also be called and can become doves. I say it again, it is he who moves beside the springs of water, giving life to faith, making fear holy, illuminating knowledge, spreading piety abroad. By the gift of the spirit of Jesus, these other doves also move beside the waters. From faith they draw life into themselves, for the just man lives by faith.* From fear they draw a holiness, not short-lived but secure, for the fear of the Lord is holy, enduring for ever.* From knowledge they draw light. The unfolding of your words gives light.* From piety they draw a heart of lovely compassion, as it is written: 'who pities and is cheerful.'* The dove hovers over the waters by bringing forth living waters from the stream which is itself. The other doves hover over the waters by

Rm 1:17

Ps 19:9

Ps 119:130

Rm 12:8

thirsting for the fountain of life and by looking for those same living waters nowhere but in that living fountain. The dove hovers over the waters by brooding over his gifts, and with the tenderness and care of a mother creating and cherishing them in those who are his children by grace. The doves hover over the waters by steadfastly cleaving to what they have received from heaven, and most watchfully fostering it within them. The Holy Spirit hovers over the springs of water, his blessing makes them stream, and in the stream he drenches them, as scripture
Ps 65:9 says: 'Saturate his rivers, multiply his seeds.'*
The doves also hover over the springs of water, pouring these same heavenly waters into themselves, streaming them abroad and
Cf. Pr 5:16 leading them through the streets.* For by
this great gift of the Holy Spirit they received not only a share in these same waters but also the office of dispensing them to the entire church of God.

So the doves hovered over the waters by being able to share them, by being watchful to preserve them and by persevering in spreading them abroad. Of their power there is no question, for he has made them princes
Ps 45:16 over all the earth,* and your friends are ex-
ceedingly honored, O God, their rule is firmly
Ps 139:17 established.* It is likewise with concern for
the leadership which rested on the shoulder of those who bore and, we hope, still bears con-
Cf. 2 Co 11:28 cern for all the churches.* Evident, too, is the
effect of their perseverence and labor. Today the generation of the saints, their descen-
Cf. Si 44:12 dants,* is as numerous as the stars of

heaven,* and from the very smallest of seeds, the pastures of the wilderness flourish, even to this day, and the hills are girded with joy.* Everywhere, the valleys of the earth are rich with corn.* So now, by copious inpouring, a few tiny brooks have become rivers; indeed, a mighty deluge has made the rivers too overflow, and they have flooded out into all that was barren and dry.

Cf. Dt 1:10

Ps 65:12

Ps 65:13

5. However, before these rivulets could be channeled off by the doves and before the doves could rest beside full flowing streams, the spirit of Jesus decided they must be washed anew. They were indeed washed once for the forgiveness of their sins at the time of their first calling. They were washed a second time when with indescribable humility—an example of humility that will never be equalled—Jesus girded himself with a towel and washed their feet, cleansing their desires of all impurity.* Jesus washed them yet again when he was about to ascend into heaven, reproaching them for the incredulity and hardness of their hearts.* Finally, he washed them when he took his seat at the right hand of the Father and poured out upon them clean water,* great quantities of it, baptizing them in the Holy Spirit.* The first washing was in the blood of Christ, for we who are baptized, were baptized in his death.* The second washing was in the humility of Christ, persuasive in its power to bend the affections of the human heart. The third washing was the sweet and gentle reproach of Jesus. The fourth and last was the generous and overwhelming outpouring of love. So the first

Cf. Jn 13:5

Cf. Mk 16:14

Cf. Ez 36:25

Cf. Mt 3:11

Rm 6:3

cleansing was in blood, the second in water, the third in milk and the fourth in wine, as it is written, 'He will wash his robe in wine.'* Gn 49:11

6. However, it is with the washing in milk that this sermon is now concerned, so let us look at the nature of this milk; let us see if we can experience its sweetness, even through one tiny drop. What, really, is this milk? What kind of thing is it? For my part, I can only believe it is no other than that which flows from the breasts of Jesus. For Jesus does have breasts. We know this from her who has seen, has caught the scent, has sucked—no, rather, has drunk deep—from the breasts of his consolation. Drinking of his sweetness, a bold excess of greater hope has grown within her, and passionate with the growing sweetness of her love, she has exclaimed: 'Let him kiss me with the kiss of his mouth, for your breasts are better than wine, more fragrant than the richest ointments.'* Sg 1:1

O how sweet this milk is, how radiantly white, how fruitful, how rich! There is this, too, that Jesus milks his breasts vigorously for the benefit of those whom he has undertaken to nurse as a special work of his favor. Like the tenderest nurse, he carries them in his arms and rests them on his breasts, so much so that he not only feeds them lovingly with his milk, but he washes them as well. How tenderly that most genuine of foods flows up from the depths of the being! How wonderfully it liquifies into milk! It is flowing in the breasts, it is drawn as milk onto the lips, it is taken drop by drop into the mouth, it is passed on to the throat, it is digested interiorly, it becomes part of the substance of a new man. It is drawn from the breasts so freely, it flows out so lavishly, it flows in so easily! How delightful its effect, how health-giving its refreshment, how inexplicable, how marvellous its fulfillment!

7. Perhaps you are waiting to hear from me exactly what these breasts of Jesus are, and what is meant by the milk of those breasts, but another has already answered for me in the past. Why should you want to hear the same thing repeated?* If anyone has forgotten it, let him ask his father and he will tell him!* The greatest triumph of our father was to write about this marriage canticle.* It was certainly granted him to speak from experience, and the more ineffable his experience of the mystery of that most sacred kiss, the more incomparable his descriptions. He ran, drawn by the scent of those sweet-smelling breasts, but we run drawn by the fragrance of his scent, and it is not so much that we run as follow after as best we can, limping along with a stick! We embrace his footprints with affection, hoping to be worthy even to touch them! However, with all respect to the mystery of those senses which he, a man powerful in word and deed, so copiously revealed from the great riches of his wisdom and eloquence, we too would like to venture some remarks, since the occasion arises. Jesus' breasts are: charity forming his little ones and charity also supporting them.

Cf. Jn 9:27

Cf. Dt 32:7

**A graceful reference to St Bernard's commentaries on the Song of Songs.*

'Charity', says the apostle, 'is patient, is kind.'* Both forms of charity are indispensable in the rearing of children, a condescen-

1 Co 13:4

sion to their weakness and a sweetness of discourse to teach them all things.* Or, if you would prefer me to put it this way, the breasts of the Incarnate Word are the goodness and loving kindness of God our Savior.* In this sense Incarnate Truth swelled, as if, as it were, into maternal breasts, rounding them out and filling them with nourishment for the little ones for whose sake he had come from heaven. He gathered together as in two flasks all the waters of that great and spacious sea,* the unsearchable riches of his goodness and wisdom.

Cf. 1 Jn 2:27

Tt 3:4

Cf. Ps 103:25

And since he could speak to them only as men of flesh not spirit, he was willing to suit himself to their childishness and to assign to them in due time not a measure of corn but a sip of milk, nourishing them thus with his goodness and instructing them in the learning of his kindness. Performing the duty of a nurse, he fed them with his own milk by himself, from himself, and lastly for himself.

So at the time for weaning, during the two days of the Lord's passion, the breasts were taken away from them, and instead of the nourishment of milk, a draft of gall and wormwood was mixed for them. At once the eyes of Jesus, and they are themselves these eyes, grew weak through lack of food. But on the third day their mother, truly a mother who does not forget the sons of her womb,* rose up early in the morning to give milk to her children, and he set before them also some more solid food, unleavened bread and a pascal lamb. So from that day on he accustomed them to more solid food and gradually with-

Cf. Ps 87:5

drew the milk, yet he did not take it away completely all at once. In turn he granted and withheld his presence in the flesh (though now a more than bodily presence) like an eagle flying back and forth, and thus tempting her chicks to fly,* so that they might learn to forget their nest and relish maturer pleasures. And since in a brief space of time they had to be completely weaned, and had already grown in size and capacity, he pressed out more abundantly the milk of his breasts so that they might be washed in it as well as fed. *Dt 32:11*

8. It was in this way that he washed the disciples on their way to Emmaus, Thomas, Peter and finally the eleven as they were at table. All of them he washed clean so as to leave not the slightest stain in his eyes, for of them it is written that 'he guarded them like the apple of his eye'.* The effect of this milk, both in restoring and in cleansing, could not be hidden by those who experienced it. 'Was our heart not burning within us,' they said, 'when he spoke to us on the way?'* Jesus reproached their foolishness and slowness of heart, the reproach wounded, the wound brought health. Their hunger he assuaged with food, their childishness be coerced with milk, he washed away the stains of unbelief, but it was a washing with milk, in a torrent of sweetness. When Thomas hardened his heart against the healing of his own wounds (of lack of faith), Jesus showed his own wounds letting him touch them with hand and fingers as he pleased, so that he might find the surest motives for belief destined to heal any similar *Dt 32:10* *Lk 24:32*

Cf. Jn 20:27 wound of incredulity in times to come.*
So he, too, was baptized in this laver of milk
and the flood of his washing has streamed out
onto us also, onto us who do not see, and
Cf. Jn 20:29 still believe.*

Then there was Peter, whose triple denial
was washed away in milk from those same
breasts when he was thrice questioned about
Cf. Jn 21:15 his love.* As if to redeem his sin, the pastoral
office was laid upon him, and a triple com-
mand urged him diligently to pasture his
sheep. The Lord did not want to reproach
him openly with the disgrace of his denial, but
to imply it almost with diffidence. 'When you
were younger,' he says, 'you girded yourself
Jn 21:18 and walked where you pleased.'* How gra-
Ps 111:3 cious and merciful the Lord is!* He washes
away the stain, and with what gentleness! He
does not chide the man he washes but makes
excuses for him. He tells him in advance how
he will glorify God in his death, and that in
the manner of his death he was destined to be
conformed to Christ the Lord.

Finally, at his last appearance, he washed
all his doves, plunging them, as it were, into a
milk bath. He blessed them once washed, and
that blessing was his farewell. He commanded
them 'to be at rest near full flowing streams,'
to sit waiting in the city until strength
Cf. Lk 24:49 should be given them from on high.* And
truly they did remain without moving, for
their expectation was firm, their hope calm
and their faith steadfast. They sat quietly like
'doves beside springs of water'; they sat
'bathed in milk', yet from the wine cellar of
the spouse they awaited gifts yet more

wonderful and abundant. Being fully weaned now and spiritual in their nature, they yearned with deepest longing for the more solid food from heaven. Since they could not follow Christ bodily as he rose into the skies, they strove to follow him in their heart and fly after him in their desires.

9. Meanwhile all their effort was to become worthy of the promise of the Spirit, the Paraclete. They awaited his coming with complete confidence and with an ever greater urgency of prayer, with immense desire, with sighs and groans. It was only right that a gift of such exceeding greatness should be poured out only on those who sighed and longed for it. Among the last words of the honeysweet blessing that Jesus gave them when he said farewell and was taken up into heaven was the final command they received from him: 'Stay in the city, until you are clothed with power from on high.'* They stayed, therefore, in the city, in the charity of the new Jerusalem. While the old Jerusalem was already collapsing about them, the new Jerusalem was being built from them, as a city, an image of that great heavenly city which is firmly bound together.* Already the Holy Spirit was at work building up this city with like stones and mortar so that God might be recognized in its houses and seen in his glory.* There was certainly a unity of purpose in this city where all shared the one utterance and had the same mind towards God and each other. For, they were all together in one place.* All together, because of their united hearts; all in one place, because of their patience. There was

Lk 24:49

Ps 122:3

Cf. Ps 48:13

Ac 2:1

union in the deepest charity and in the fellowship of the spirit, there was patience in the long, submissive waiting for the Holy Spirit. Anything that might be a stumblingblock to charity, had already been banished far from that city. Very far away from those despisers of the world was any dispute about worldly matters, infinitely remote from those votaries of humility all that old quarrel as to which
Lk 22:24 was greater.* Now it was the reverse, the only dispute concerned who should be the less, who should be the servant of all, and who should be the last, who should be the more submissive. Form your own opinion: were they not 'at rest near full flowing streams', who were preparing themselves like this to drink of them?

10. The 'full flowing streams', moreover, are the four rivers of grace: fortitude, counsel, understanding, and wisdom. A mighty spring, arising from the middle of paradise, a vein of living waters did the Holy Spirit divide into these four rivers, especially at that time when, coming with a violent surge, he glad-
Cf. Ps 46:4 dened the city of God* and filled the whole
Ac 2:2 house where they were seated.*

Then in a spirit of fortitude he strengthens
Cf. Ps 147:13 the bars of the gates of Jerusalem,* and builds
Is 5:2 a tower in the midst of her,* a tower of
Ps 61:3 fortitude in the face of the foe.* From that day forth the Lord has set them like a horse coming down to the field of glory, surefooted, sniffing the battle from afar. He presses on quickly to meet the warriors, and when he hears the trumpet sound, he says:
Cf. Jb 39:25 'Aha!'* The Lord of hosts is with us, and

who is against us?* From the spirit of counsel they drink in counsel and prudence, so that their city is not only furnished with horses and arms but also invincible in its battle leaders and the wise counsel of its elders. Fortitude is indeed a horse, and a strong one, ready for the day of battle, but it is a vain hope for safety* if not controlled by the restraining spirit of counsel. If fortitude is to remain unconquered, let it take for rider the spirit of counsel, and under its guiding rein let it come down into the field, prepared for fighting. Zechariah is our witness that: 'What reins in the horse will be holy to the Lord.'* It is the spirit of counsel he is referring to, for when that is absent, the horse stumbles, and behind him his rider also falls.* Just as they became brave and strong through the spirit of fortitude, so they became wise and prudent through the spirit of counsel, choosing cautiously for the most part to avoid danger to save themselves for the greater good of the church. Nor did they think it right to hasten their own glory at the cost of causing harm to the many, for they had been instructed by the Holy Spirit in the laws of charity to seek not their own good but that of others.*

Cf. Ps 46:7,11

Cf. Ps 33:17

Zc 14:20

Cf. Gn 49:17

Cf. 1 Co 13:5

11. From the spirit of understanding they received a great book, the whole of God's creation, and there, as he opened and unfolded it they read of the goodness and wisdom of God; under his guidance they learned of his power and greatness through the things he had made.* The same spirit kept constantly before their eyes in the words and deeds of Jesus a book of easier understanding.

Cf. Rm 1:20

As it is written of him: 'The Holy Spirit whom the Father shall send in my name,' he says, 'he will teach you all things and bring to your minds whatever I have said to you.'*

Jn 14:26

Strengthened by this spirit, they bore with equanimity the loss of Christ in the flesh, doubtless understanding the meaning of that saying: 'It is expedient to you that I go away.'*

Jn 16:7

So this spirit calmed and enlightened their whole understanding, so that the spirit of wisdom might then enkindle and strengthen their will. For by the spirit of wisdom charity takes delight in everything which the understanding sets before it. It almost seems to taste, in a heavenly and living way, what it understands, and hence to evaluate it rightly; and it spreads through each individual part of the soul, giving life to all the senses and powers. Through this spirit they were clothed with the wisdom which is from above, men of true wisdom to the extent that they savor only God and the things of God. So violent was this flood of the spirit upon them, that being unable to contain it wholly themselves, they chose to open themselves to every soul and to strive to make all those who shared their nature become a sharer in this savor. In this most loving attempt to save all men the same spirit of wisdom provided not only goodwill but a tongue also. With these burning tongues they could speak with fiery eloquence and speak the tongues of all seeing that they desired to unite all men to Christ.

As we were saying, therefore, it was beside these full flowing streams that the doves were resting. Through the ministry of these same doves, by the generous gift of the Holy Spirit, we have all received a share in their fulness according to the measure of the gift of Christ,* and he uses these same doves as his dispensers. We also are at rest near the same streams, for they intercede for us with the giver of all good things, the Holy Spirit. Restfully then we pray to the Holy Spirit, *Ep 4:7*

who with God the Father
and his holy only-begotten Son,
our Lord Jesus Christ,
lives and reigns, God,
for ever and ever.
Amen.

SERMON EIGHTEEN

The beginning of the eighteenth sermon. That, on the authority of holy scripture, seven gifts are typified by the eyes of the spouse. Why the same gifts are called doves. That, through grace, he bestows these gifts on us, and not to recognize them is no small ingratitude.

'HIS EYES are doves beside springs of
water, bathed in milk, at rest near full
Sg 5:12 flowing streams.'* 'Light is sweet,'
says Solomon, 'and it is pleasant to behold the
Qo 11:7 sun with eyes.'* How sweeter to behold the
light of the sun? The spouse is himself
Cf. Mt 17:2 light,* and his whole face shines like the sun,
yet in the eyes of this sun the force of his
beauty is exceptional, it demands our admira-
tion, and there is a kind of perpetual splendor
of light, glittering with grace. In Daniel, the
eyes of the son of man are compared to
Cf. Rv 1:14 flames of fire,* and they are described by
Cf. Gn 49:12 Jacob as more beautiful than wine.* Well
then, if they are a flame of fire, why do I not
draw near them to warm myself? If they are
wine, or more beautiful than wine, why do I
not hasten to drink? Why do you trouble this
Mt 26:10 woman,* you crowd of my cares, you tor-
menting worries, you unruly mob of thoughts,
Jb 17:11 all wasting and racking my heart?* Why do
you come before me like a cloud, so that

I cannot see the light of heaven,* and the very light of my eyes is gone from me?* Why should you be this day to me as an adversary,* and fraudulently deprive my poor little soul of the eyes of Jesus, more beautiful than wine? Depart from me, you evildoers,* and then I may be able to pluck for myself some small happiness, even if only passing. If the blessing of sight is beyond me, at least allow me eagerness for sight, a fervent longing for it. So great is the merit of this beauty that scripture rightly said of it that the longing for it leads to a kingdom.* Therefore, the mere desire of this beauty brings with it the putting off of our native ugliness and clothes us with a large share of beauty. I will go, then, and with all the strength I can muster, I will try to tear myself free from the crowd that presses and oppresses me. I am small in stature, so I will climb into some tree, where I may at least see the face of Jesus as he passes by.* I will at least catch sight of the face he wears now as he comes to visit his wandering exiles.

Cf. Tb 11:8
Ps 38:10
2 S 19:22
Ps 119:115
Cf. Ws 6:21
Cf. Lk 19:3-5

2. I recall, in fact, a man who was blessed with a longing for this kind of vision, and he grew suddenly to such a stature that he enjoyed the sight of Jesus at will. He was able to receive him with joy as he came nearer and nearer, to act as his host, to possess him as an intimate companion. Others, too, burning with the same desire, though as yet gentiles and sinners, I remember as having said to Philip: 'Master, we desire to see Jesus.'* Surely these also were men of low stature, and by the measure of the age which is in

Jn 12:21

Christ Jesus, they were perhaps the least of all. Deliberately, then, they climbed a tree, to see Jesus. Thereupon Philip went to Andrew, and Andrew, together with Philip, was found to be a faithful messenger of this holy desire with Jesus. It was a loving desire, and Jesus responded lovingly. 'The hour has come,' he said, 'for the son of man to be
Jn 12:23 glorified.'* For it is true that if a man ardently seeks the sight of Jesus, he has come himself in this hour to glorify the son of man, he has gone already to the feast, for
Cf. Jn 7:10 him the day of festivity has already dawned.*

Scripture says of those gentiles that they went up to Jerusalem to worship at the
Jn 12:20 feast.* So this is a sign to you that you have seen Jesus, if you have glorified him, praising and blessing him with all your heart, if the sight has filled you with wonder, confusion, emotion, if all the arrogance of your heart has melted like wax before his glory, if, finally, you have feasted and exulted at the
Cf. Ps 68:4 sight of him and are jubilant with joy,* your whole heart rejoicing in him, because your
Cf. Lk 2:30 eyes have seen the salvation of God.* O face more desirable than anything else, never holding yourself back from those who seek you, and glorifying with your own light those who see you!

Yet as is said here by Jesus himself, this festivity and glory only takes place for an hour, and that hour is very brief and exceptionally rare. 'The hour has come,' he says,
Jn 12:23 'for the son of man to be glorified.'* But happy the hour and weighty the business of this hour, in which he in turn gives glory to

those who glorify him. Lord God of hosts, convert us, show us your face and we shall be saved.* The sight of the face of Jesus truly *Ps 80:19*
saves us, truly gives life to us. No man will see him without immediately dying to himself and taking new life in him. Blessed are the eyes of the sun, and blessed are all those who have seen them.

3. Who, then, are these? In the case of lovers, it seems to me not too daring to call them wisdom and understanding. These are the eyes with which the face of Jesus is both sought with urgency and seen with happiness, for he is as it were tasted with the eye of wisdom and recognized with the eye of understanding. Of the first it is said: 'Taste and see that the Lord is sweet.'* And of the *Ps 34:8*
second: 'Give me understanding and I shall live.'* Besides, the eyes of Jesus are a gift of *Ps 119:144*
this twofold grace, the spirit of wisdom and the spirit of understanding. It is clearly impossible for Jesus to be seen by any eye, unless Jesus first looks down from heaven, and by his look brings that eye into existence. In both these graces, Jesus acts before his lover can act. By infusing the sense of his goodness, he disposes to wisdom, and by giving a perception of his truth, he illumines the heart through understanding. Perhaps it is because of this double gift of grace that the way he sees is shown in the psalms as something recurring. 'From heaven,' it says, 'the Lord looked down, and he saw all the sons of men.'* And again: 'He looked down from *Ps 33:13*
his holy height, from heaven the Lord beheld the earth.'* Therefore, 'O Lord God of hosts, *Ps 102:19*

turn again, look down from heaven and see,
Ps 80:14 visit this vineyard.'* 'Look down and see'—by your twofold glance, give us those blessed eyes, and form in us that double grace by the frequency of your glance.

4. In the face of Jesus, therefore, as was said above, there are two eyes, but there are nevertheless seven eyes altogether. For he is that living stone of whom it is written in Zechariah, that in that single stone were seven
Cf. Zc 3:9 eyes.* He is also that true lamb which John saw to have seven eyes. He explains their significance by saying: 'which are the seven
Rv 5:6 spirits of God sent out into all the earth.'* It is then a sevenfold spirit that the Father sends
Cf. Jn 14:26 in the name of Jesus* on all who believe in the name of Jesus, and whom Jesus sends from the Father. And the spirit himself, blowing
Cf. Jn 3:7 when he will and as he will,* he himself is the light of Jesus' eyes. Of him it is written: 'Learn where there is wisdom, where there is understanding, that you may at the same time discern where there is length of days and life, where there is light for the eyes and
Cf. Ba 3:14 peace.'*

These are, therefore, the blessed and beatific eyes which he raised on his disciples to bless them, when he said: 'Blessed are the
Mt 5:4 meek,'* and the other things which he added, opening his mouth to heap blessing upon blessing. These seven gifts the good worker so teaches as to give, so utters as to imprint, and so discreetly introduces as to fill our hearts with them as he makes them known. This is why we must call master on earth only him who alone is master in heaven as

well. Only he is able to teach by the sweetness of his utterance alone, and if he deigns to make men his disciples, he also makes them docile to his teaching.

5. So it is obvious why the bride has described the eyes of her beloved as doves, since in the scriptures, the most usual name for the Holy Spirit is dove, and since his grace is sevenfold, doves are spoken of in the plural. If a justification is sought for this name, there is a sort of sevenfold grace to be met with in this species of bird. It builds its nest in the topmost edge of the gorge, as it is written,* *Cf. Jr 48:28* and by this seems to form us to poverty and in a certain sense to tell us: 'Blessed are the poor in spirit.'* *Mt 5:3* Then it yields without rebellion or the desire for revenge on anyone, even on someone smaller than itself, who wants to drive it out of its poor little dwelling place, and by this it seems to say to us: 'Blessed are the meek.'* *Mt 5:4* It sighs persistently, never ceasing, never wearied, and this can be taken as crying to us: 'Blessed are those who mourn.'* *Mt 5:5* It flies with the swiftest wing to eat and drink, and if other food is wanting, will even take sand for its meal, thus in a certain sense inviting us to the true food and drink, saying: 'Blessed are those who hunger and thirst after justice.'* *Mt 5:6* It is incessantly occupied with warming and feeding its young, and so seems as if encouraging us to compassion, saying: 'Blessed are the merciful.'* *Mt 5:7* Not infrequently it is grievously tormented by hunger, and yet it holds aloof from any acts of prey or from carrion; it will only take food that is pure and, as it were, urges purity upon us, saying:

Mt 5:8 'Blessed are the pure in heart.'* It lives happily with birds of its own species and is glad to be one of a community, mixing with them not only without friction but with positive affec-
Cf. Ps 120:6 tion; even with those who hate peace* it conducts itself peacefully, and by this appears to be preaching peace to us, saying: 'Blessed
Mt 5:9 are the peacemakers.'*

These, then, are the seven eyes of the lamb
Rv 5:6 without spot.* These are the seven spirits which, having ascended to heaven and sat down at the right hand of the Father, he sent into the whole earth, distributing them in whatever measure he wished.

6. Yet until Jesus was glorified it was neither possible nor seemly for the Holy Spirit to be poured out so generously on all the earth. It was this generous outpouring of the Spirit that was in a special way the glorification of Jesus in heaven as well as on earth. It was the sign he had ascended to his Father
Cf. Jn 20:17 and our Father,* and was quite unmistakably equal to his Father in power and in eternity, and so, as he promised before and now clearly does, he could pour out the Holy Spirit, the
Cf. Rm 8:15 Paraclete, on the sons of his adoption.* Truly he is the Christ, the chosen one of
Lk 23:35 God,* anointed Christ with all the fulness of the Holy Spirit, and able to anoint with the Spirit all whom he chooses and to the extent he chooses. How supremely high towers the glory of Jesus! It is through him that the Holy Spirit is given, and without him no one can give him and no one can receive him! Indeed, as Jesus prophesied of him, the Holy
Cf. Jn 16:14 Spirit when he came glorified Jesus,* showing

him most glorious in his coming and bearing witness by that coming to his being truly the Son of God, equal in glory to his Father.* This was also shown, but at that time in a hidden manner, when the Holy Spirit came down upon Jesus in the form of a dove and rested upon him.* Then the voice of the Father made clear John, and through him to us, that: 'this is he who baptizes in the Holy Spirit.'* He alone has the power, not only of remitting sins in the Holy Spirit, but of pouring out an ever-increasing flood of grace, which he himself describes as baptism in the Holy Spirit when he says: 'You will all be baptized in the Holy Spirit not many days hence.'*

Cf. Mk 15:39

Cf. Jn 1:32

Jn 1:33

Ac 1:5

So when the dove had found a home for itself, and a sure and lovely dwelling, it then wanted a firm and clean place to launch itself. But while it took flight it nonetheless remained there, showing that the Spirit blows where Jesus wishes and that it comes from him and returns to him. It gives proofs of its coming and that no eye can mistake, renewing the face of the earth, and wherever it comes making a new creation. In one moment it makes sons of God out of sons of iniquity, and from the cleft in any wall, however sloping and ruinous, the dove can freely cry to the Father of the Lord Jesus: 'Abba, Father!'*

Rm 8:15

No longer can the waters of human affection, though by nature fickle and flowing by natural inclination to the sea, pursue their accustomed course, because the eyes of Jesus, like doves, are now at rest beside the springs of water. Neither the spirit of the flesh nor the spirit of this world now broods over them,

and these waters are not themselves accustomed to breathe out this kind of impurity, for the Spirit of the Lord, the Spirit of truth, the Spirit of holiness, hovers above the
Cf. Gn 1:2 waters.* These waters are ever near for those who thirst, not now like the waters of Jacob's well, those who drink of which thirst again, but living waters quenching all thirst for
Cf. Jn 4:13 earthly desire.* A desire springing up to life eternal is aroused by the Holy Spirit who moves over these waters.

7. You understand what I am saying, brothers, because in your day-to-day experience you see these things within your very selves. For you have received this heavenly blessing more abundantly than many children of grace, and I hope very earnestly that this may not be said in condemnation but to encourage you to progress. I do not quite see how we are grateful to the Spirit for some of his graces, or at any rate grateful enough, if we are not able to say along with the apostle: 'But we have not received the spirit of this world, but the Spirit which is from God, that we may understand what
1 Co 2:12 has been given us from God.'*

Thanks be to God, then, for raising those blessed eyes of his also to us and by his words breathing into us the grace of poverty, freely chosen. He speaks, and by his bounty it comes to pass that we become the blessed who are
Mt 5:3 poor in spirit.* This first blessing is indeed a princely one, for, not taking into account the great reward of the kingdom which we await with certainty, what glory, what riches it is to have despised the glory and riches of the

world for the sake of Christ! In comparison with him, what things of this world do not seem unsightly and base, however much they glitter in the eyes of the foolish?

But God opened his hand still wider to pour out on us the spirit of meekness. Thus enriched we consecrated to him our hands and our will. We have become in his sight like a beast of burden, ready on his behalf to go wherever the hand of our rider leads by halter and rein. Let there be no trace of kicking against the goad,* because, quite obviously, to murmur against our teachers is to persecute Christ, not to follow him. A man like this would have to fear hearing what Paul heard: 'Why do you persecute me? It is hard for you to kick against the goad.'* How much more pleasant will resound in your soul—if you are fortunate enough to hear it—that saying of the heavenly bridegroom: I have compared you, my love to my horsemen amidst the chariots of Pharaoh. We were set among the chariots of Pharaoh when we were the slaves of sin and free from the claim of righteousness; by sin in the eyes of the law, were the volunteers of Pharaoh, and indeed the foes of righteousness. But now likened by Christ in his compassion to his own horsemen, we have become like the meekest of asses, having Christ as our rider and guide, and, having submitted to a far greater obedience, for the power of him whom we serve is incomparably greater, it behooves us to be still more fervent and prompt in our readiness to obey. Indeed, by the help of God, by this first gift of the Spirit we overcome the

Cf. Ac 26:14

Ibid.

world, but by this second gift—something far more astonishing—we learn to place our own selves under subjection.

Moreover, when God blesses us, he blesses us in the fullest sense of the word, and at the right time the water of tears comes to bedew
Cf. Ps 144:12 his young plants.* They may be tears for the blunders we grieve to have committed in the past, when we were in Pharaoh's chariots, or for those blunders we still make, to our shame, everyday in many different ways. They may be tears because we can scarcely lift up our head for disgrace and distress when we consider the standards of our fathers and the ways of old, or because, after wrestling with our temptations, we have been defeated and in ignominy have deserted the field of battle, or because—and these tears are happier—we are mourning the sadness and tedious duration of our life in exile. At this point I am reminded for the moment of the five gates of the pool where the angel of the Lord used to descend
Cf. Jn 5:4 to heal the sick and the enfeebled.* Obviously, when he came, he did not descend in vain, nor was the water stirred without some effect, for Jesus certainly does not despise a humble and
Ps 51:17 contrite heart.* It was to console those who mourn that he came, and to give them 'the oil
Cf. Is 61:3 of gladness in exchange for mourning.'*

Is this not a very great grace, my brothers? It makes satisfaction for the evils of the past and it is a remedy against the evils of the present, and it obviates the evils of the future. Sanctification is in its gift, and with its encouraging strength we are made ready to receive it.

8. Having eaten, therefore of the bread of tears* and drunk of their cup, we are im- *Cf. Ps 80:5* mediately overwhelmed with a new blessing. We are refreshed by the Spirit of life with a bread very much stronger, more of a delicacy, with a keener relish to it, and having once eaten it, we never cease to hunger for it. This is the bread that says of itself: 'Those who eat me will hunger for more.'* *Si 24:21* For no one can even feel hunger for him, unless he has first given of himself to a man's mouth. It is by this generous blessing of the Lord of Hosts, that I see you competing in spirited rivalry for the better gifts;* *Cf. 1 Co 12:31* I see you instant in prayer, watchful in vigils, mortified at table, secluded and silent, spiritually on fire for acts of righteousness. I see you eating of this bread, and after you have eaten, hungering for it, as if you were already beginning to sit with Jesus at his table and feast on the bread that he breaks.

Enriched as you are with the bread of righteousness, the Lord has also not held back from you the grace of a merciful heart. You are eager to share your righteousness willingly and gladly with those who have not obtained it for themselves. In fact, if you rebuke one another, or if there is mutual accusation [in chapter], I am convinced you do this out of a compassionate zeal for the good, and I long very earnestly for you to be no less convinced of it among yourselves. It seems to me fitting that I should think this about all of you, and that all of you should think this about one another. If someone has shortly before given a compassionate rebuke to his brother, and

then sees him ill or depressed, surely with identical tenderness he will immediately make himself ready to perform the office of a servant? Is he not on flame at the offense of his brother, and yet also suffering with him in
Cf. 2 Co 11:29 his pain and pining with him in his misery?* This is so rich a blessing that anyone who deserves to receive it from the Lord's hand is not only blessed himself but becomes a blessing, because to abound in compassion towards your brother is to overflow with what could be called the oil of blessing.

9. But above and beyond all these, there is a blessing which is the more perfect for being more interior in that amidst all the blessings I have mentioned it purifies the intention of the heart from all the leaven of the
Lk 12:1 Pharisees, which is hypocrisy.* It guards it from the least touch of dishonor, like the
Cf. Ps 17:8 apple of its eye.* Endowed with this blessing, a man will live securely in the house of the Lord, the house, that is to say, of a pure conscience which he enters without a stain. In the morning he destroys all the wicked of the
Cf. Ps 101:8 land,* a rigorous judge and dread avenger of every evil thought. It is through the favor of this blessing that you so frequently show yourselves to the priest, merciless to your sense of dignity or shame, and that you hasten, with kind severity, to dash against a
Cf. Ps 137:9 stone the little ones of Babylon,* not yet grown to the size of a man's hand.

10. Last of all, the Lord our God has blessed his people, and we are that people,
Cf. Ps 29:11 with peace,* and not with one kind of peace but with two. There is the peace we have among ourselves and from ourselves to

all men, and there is the peace we have with God. It is our duty carefully to guard both kinds of peace, and to put them to good use with real earnestness. We must see to it that we take away even the least stone that might make us stumble on the road of peace where, by the mercy of God, we are walking, and each one of us must take all possible measures, as the apostle says, to please his brother so as to edify him.* *Cf. Rm 15:2* In this peace, our designs and desires find their joyful perfection, so that the peace of Christ exults in our hearts,* *Cf. Col 3:15* and peace is perfected by peace, and we take our delight in the great, satisfying richness of our present peace.

Blessed be the Lord our God, who has blessed us with manifold blessings, and day by day extends these blessings and makes them more glorious. But there is one thing which we have very greatly to fear, that the vessel of our longing desire, which we can hold up to be filled by that rich and liberal giver, may turn out to be too small, and so the oil will cease to flow,* *Cf. 2 K 4:6* the vessel being inadequate. Yet if we are wise, we will wait and pray, hopefully and perseveringly, not just for oil and the blessing of oil, but for vessels, too, and a sufficiency of them, because of the inexhaustible generosity of him who,

with God the Father and the Holy Spirit,
lives and reigns, God,
for ever and ever.
Amen.

SERMON NINETEEN

The beginning of the nineteenth sermon. Of the different ways the Lord Jesus has of regarding. What are rivulets of water, and why they are not springs but rivulets. Of the nature of the milk in which the Holy Spirit is washed, and that it is ordained to holiness as well as to delight. What are the full flowing streams, near which the doves are said to be at rest.

I FIND IT DIFFICULT, brothers, to let myself be wrenched away from the sight of those eyes, so infinitely to be desired. But I fear also some obstacle in your own fatigue, lest perhaps you find it difficult to bear this reluctance of mine. But I appeal to that knowledge you share among you, which has deserved even once to enjoy this sight, to bear witness how good it is to be attached to it, how wholesome it is to lose oneself in it, how full of gladness it is to lose oneself utterly in it. To rest your strength on it is to stand firm; to lose yourself in it is to be more and more enlightened; to cleave to it will be finally to be made like to it, to be made one with it. To look at those eyes is to have received a promise of grace; to be looked at by them in turn is to have received grace itself, here and now. In a word, nobody is holy, nobody is or can be just or good if he has not found grace in those eyes. Those eyes are full of grace, or, better put, they are themselves the fulness of grace, because a look from them suffices for every inpouring or confirming of grace in the sons of grace. But those eyes have many different ways of looking and they apportion the work of salvation according to the various reasons that make it necessary. To sum up, Jesus from the shore beheld Peter and Andrew, as well as James and John,* and he drew them from the restless waves of this present life to the shore of the sea, that is, to contempt of the world. *Cf. Jn 21:4*

2. On the mountain, accordingly, he lifted up his eyes to them and their fellow disciples and called them, by his words in their ears and his grace in their hearts, to greater heights of virtue.* At the beginning of his passion, when he was already taking his place in the courtroom, he looked at Peter;* the sacrament of our redemption was already under way, and he was preparing Peter in advance for the penance and pardon that would flow from it. From the cross he looked at his crucifiers and at all who were guilty of shedding his most sacred blood, (I shrink to say and I dread not to admit that at sometime we too have been among them). From the cross then he looked at all us sinners, fastening our sins to his cross and pleading with his Father for transgressors, that they might not perish.* From heaven he looked at his disciples, gathered together into one, when he poured out upon them the abundance of his Spirit and created from them new heavens for his *Cf. Lk 6:20* *Cf. Lk 22:61* *Cf. Is 53:12*

delight. From them, also, as if from his holy throne, he looked down on all who dwell on
Ps 33:14 the earth,* and he poured out his Spirit upon all flesh through their hands, drenching them with sacred unction.

Indeed, even before these glances of his, when he was still in his most holy and hidden resting place, the bosom of the Father, he looked on the lowliness of his handmaid, whom rightly they call blessed and all gen-
Lk 1:48 erations shall call her so.* For she found grace most richly in his eyes, and not for herself only, but for all the generations which
Cf. Est 7:3 are to come.* From the bosom of the Father, Jesus saw the one to whom, by an unique and irrevocable privilege, he gave the name of mother, so that he who was the son of the Most High was also the son of his most lowly handmaid. The Lord is high, and from his
Cf. Ps 138:6 height he looks on the lowly,* all the more because by his unchangeable decree everyone
Cf. Lk 18:14 who humbles himself will be exalted.*

Now, if I am not mistaken, it is clear to you why the eyes of the spouse are said to be like doves beside rivulets of water. You can see that it is only on the small and lowly that Jesus looks or the Spirit rests.

3. The dove loves the rivulets of water and frequents them with joy, but in the flood of many waters she cannot find a place to set
Cf. Gn 8:9 her foot.* So, if you want to have the Holy Spirit dwelling within you and ever present to console you, then you must be a rivulet, that is, you must be a little one. You must be a rivulet, and always bear in mind that you flow forth from the fountain. But if this slips your

memory, beware that you do not become dry or rather, beware lest you have become dry already! You must be careful to remember that you have nothing which you have not received,* and that it is from the free, boundless flow of the fountain that your waters spring. If you long to swell the flow of this water do not imagine it more than a trickle. 'You looked for abundance,' it says, 'and see, it came to little.'* So if you want to look for the Holy Spirit in abundance, if your desire is to abound in the Holy Spirit, then always keep an eye on your own littleness and be anxiously conscious of your deficiencies. Believe me, thoughts like these are a proof of rich plenty to come, just as, on the contrary, to have your eye always on your own abundance is an infallible prognostic of sterility and want. Why did such a great famine rage long ago in Egypt, if not because such great fertility had gone before? Each one was saying in the abundance of his heart: I shall see no want for ever. And then, all of a sudden, those who were full before have hired themselves out for bread.*

Cf. 1 Cor 4:7

Hg 1:9

1 S 2:5

It is for this very reason that we see in our own day that from the secret recesses of his grace the Holy Spirit breaks the font of living waters into streams and torrents, and yet, nonetheless, in his secret judgement he dries up the rivers of Etham.* 'He turns rivers into a desert, springs of water into thirsty ground.'*

Cf. Ps 74:15 (Vulg.)

Ps 107:33

If anything of that heavenly light has shone on your eyes, be careful not to vaunt yourself on it as though you had escaped all the

darkness of being blind. Do not let your speech make you into one of those who rebelled against the Light by claiming: 'Surely
Jn 9:40 we are not blind?'* What you must do rather is to listen to the Light, and submit humbly when he says to you: 'For a little longer the Light is with you. So while you have the Light, believe in the Light, that you may be
Jn 12:35-36 sons of Light.'* Blessed be God, who has
2 Co 4:6 given us a light to shine out of the darkness!* But if we say that we have a great light in us, when really it is only a little light, we would have to fear that what was little would shrink from littleness to nothingness, and in a little while become darkness. If we would be worthy of being sons of light, then we must bewail the darkness which still closes us in on every side. If we are not to be blind, then we must feel no shame in admitting that, in fact, we are blind.

There is great merit in God's eyes when a man sees his blindness, sees it, bitterly laments it, and takes it to Jesus to be healed. Do you want to know how great that merit is? 'If you were blind,' says Jesus, 'you would have no sin. But since you say that you can see, your
Jn 9:41 sin stands.'* And again: 'For judgement I have come into this world, that those who do not see, may see, and that those who do see, may
Jn 9:39 become blind.'* What a true judgement this is and how truly justified in itself! It is wholly just in its obvious fairness, that those who confess their blindness and lament it, should be the ones to escape into the country of light, while those who boast that they can see, though they are blind, should be the

ones to stumble into a country where the gloom is still heavier. So by the judgement of Jesus and by his stretching out his hand in blessing, those who are blind see, and those who see become blind. 'Go back to John,' he said, 'and tell him what you have seen and heard. The blind see, the deaf hear, lepers are cleansed, the lame walk, the dead rise, the poor have the gospel preached to them.'* *Mt 11:4-5*

4. These miracles are extraordinarily great and marvelous. Only Jesus could do such things, and only John or someone like John could really appreciate their wonder. If I am not mistaken, Jesus made clear to his servant, the nature of the rivulets of water on which he keeps his eyes and on which, in consequence, his Spirit rests. In short, he is the one who is spoken of in Isaiah as breaking down our deafness and flashing gloriously upon our blindness: 'Hear, you deaf, and look, you blind, that you may see!'* *Is 42:18* To these words he adds: 'Who is so blind as my servant, who so deaf as those to whom I send my messenger?'* *Is 42:19*

Obviously, what is said in the first place about blindness is meant to be applied to all the other kinds of suffering which come next. Recognition of the truth and grief for it release the captives from their chains, and, in a very wonderful way, they are free men in exact proportion as they grieve that they are captive. The more they grieve at being captive, the more they are released from their captivity.* *Cf. Ps 102:20* Surely it was a man with good sight of whom it was said: 'Light has arisen for the just'?* Yet surely he was still blind

Ps 18:28 who said: 'My God, enlighten my darkness'?* Must it not have been a man of good hearing who said: 'I will hear what the Lord God
Ps 85:8 speaks within me'* and 'Speak, Lord, for
1 S 3:9 your servant is listening'?* On the other hand, is he not deaf who often closes his ears to the suggestions of evil spirits, and so becomes 'like a man who does not hear and in
Ps 38:14 whose mouth is no reply'?* In the same way, they are certainly clean of whom it was said: 'You are clean now on account of the word I
Jn 15:3 have spoken to you.'* Yet they are more truly and deeply clean when they say: 'We have all become like one who is unclean, and all that integrity of ours is like filthy cloth-
Is 64:6 ing.'* The man who says, and can say it in all sincerity: 'You widened the path beneath
Ps 18:36 my feet, and my steps did not falter,'* that man is certainly pressing forward strongly and speedily. But if the time comes when he
Ps 94:18 knows how to say: 'My foot slipped,'* and
Jb 6:13 'Can any power be found within myself?'*, then Jesus has blessed him. This means that the lame man will have the springing step of a stag, but if the touch of Jesus makes him,
Cf. Gn 32:31 like Jacob, realize that his gait halts,* then wisdom is not lacking in him.

Furthermore, those who have eternal life, which is Christ Jesus, dwelling within them are the only ones who are truly alive. Nevertheless, there are the people who hear from the apostle: 'You have died, and your life is
Col 3:3 hid with Christ in God.'* As the same apostle says, the body indeed has died on account of sin, which holds it bound in the inevitable necessity of death, but the spirit is

alive, on account of justification.* So by some ineffable miracle, these men are beginning to invigorate their dead selves with eternal life, seeing that they live while they are nevertheless dead, and they are dead while they are still alive. *Cf. Rm 8:10*

But last of all, as if specially great and important, there is added this, that: 'the poor have the gospel preached to them.'* This brings us back again to the same sense of marvelous paradox. For when it says the gospel is preached this way [to them as poor], it is as if to say they are declared rich. *Mt 11:5*

5. What can be richer than to be established as kings of the kingdom of heaven, not in the sense of depending on some hope still to come, but in actual daily possession of its richness? Of them it is said that already, 'theirs is the kingdom of heaven.'* But again, what can be poorer than to be allowed to have absolutely nothing of this world's goods and to have barely an infinitesimal foretaste of that heavenly kingdom? What kind of kings are they, except in the way that David was a king? Kings indeed, anointed with chrism, and yet they are desperately in need. I would describe them as possessing nothing except a shepherd's bag. *Mt 5:3*

And so, in this present time, every single blessing that comes to us from the hand of Jesus falls short of perfection. Otherwise we might perhaps pride ourselves, as if we had already arrived or were already perfect, instead of straining forward, eager to lay hold of perfection one way or another.* If we compare our vision in this life, however clear it is, to the sight of that eternal light, in which *Cf. Ph 3:12*

Cf. Ps 35:10 'light is seen in light'* by the blessed eyes of those in heaven, what is it but cloud and blindness? Here on this earth the man in whom the Lord God speaks hears in his ear a faint and very occasional whisper. What is that to the mighty roar of mighty thunder which is heard in heaven by those worthy to hear the Father speaking openly of the Son, or the Son
Cf. Jn 16:25 of the Father?* If you compare them, will you not, with good reason, call our hearing deafness? All the purity of the sons of men compared–I do not say with the holiness which is above but just compared–within your own self and laid open before the gaze of your own judgement, does it not appear foul in your own eyes and small evil to your own nostrils?

Those who run in the race, if they want to
Cf. 1 Co 9:24 run so as to lay hold of the prize,* must remember all the time that it is not a matter of 'a man willing or a man running, but of God
Rm 9:16 taking pity.'* Life here below, as far as it is lived for God, is beset with very many perils and only God holds our breath safe in his hands. Every moment it is on the brink of death, and so what is life except a picture of death? The very majesty of the kingly dignity which Christ proclaims to his poor as the gospel message, what is it but the shadow of its great name? While life lasts, these royal paupers long for the crumbs that fall from
Cf. Mt 15:27 their master's table,* and only rarely and after much begging do they get a fleeting taste of anything at all.

6. In saying this we are not voicing any criticism of the loving eyes of the spouse or

taking anything from the generosity of the Holy Spirit, as if his hand was shortened. We are insisting only that we measure correctly our slight capacity and the limits of our virtues, such as they are, for the eyes of Jesus look only on the poor and doves rest only by the little streams of water. If you are to be a true rivulet, then you must take care never to swell out and overflow your course. Follow the advice of the king of Israel: 'Be content with your glory,'* –if you must glory, which is not usually very profitable!* You will not easily succeed in flowing out and streaming beyond and above yourself without breaking your banks and drowning your neighbors' crops. If you want the font of life to be forever supplying you with water, be wary of growing too great, be wary of overflowing! If you are the Lord's bride and have been found worthy to conceive in the spirit form his joyous kisses and blessed embrace, let your soul magnify the Lord.* Never magnify your own self, not even what has been brought to birth within you by the Holy Spirit.

2 Kg 14:10
Cf. 2 Co 12:1
Cf. Lk 1:46

7. Follow the example of the most blessed of mothers and the humblest of virgins, and lay up a treasure for yourself with fresh stores of humility. In all that you do, keep her ever before you. Prepare in your heart new ways of rising on high with the Lord's mother: go down with haste, that is, go up with her into the hill country* and with the blessings of sweetness with which the Holy Spirit has greeted you, give a blessing in and from your heart, so that your brothers' hearts

Cf. Lk 1:39

may rejoice to be filled with your blessing. Take pains to be submissive even to those less important than yourself; be quick to be the first in rendering a service; be wholly intent upon giving thanks. Do these things generously, though you are ever mindful of your unimportance. Exult with joy, yet let your praise be reverent and grave. Give thanks indeed, but let there resound in them this word of lowliness: 'A little child is born
Cf. Is 35:2 to us.'*

Thanks be to you, Lord Jesus, thanks be to your Holy Spirit! All unworthy as I am, I have been granted the grace, even in a slight degree, of conceiving by him. Now your mercy must take over to foster this little seed of yours and make it grow! It would be better not to have conceived at all than for me not to cherish the Lord's seed with motherly tenderness and not to let it grow up by its rightful increase in stature. Believe me, to be affected in this way, to become yearningly conscious of Jesus in this way, is to be already endowed with a mother's heart. This is how you will draw the eyes of the beloved unwaveringly to yourself and will make a perpetual resting place for the doves beside the rivulets of water. 'But if you want even more, if you call the doves to be at rest', etc. Still more, you will invite them to rest near full-flowing waters, and await better and more perfect gifts from the Holy Spirit, but only if these doves have first been washed by you in milk to their satisfaction.

8. But, you will ask, what is meant by this bathing of the doves and where am I to find

milk for it?

If you are really the bride of the Lord and have conceived some spiritual offspring of your sacred love, then that milk is very close to you, in your heart and in your breast. Or rather, it wells from your inmost depths into your breasts. That milk is thanksgiving, with which, at the same time, Jesus is cherished and the Holy Spirit cleansed. But there is a condition: the gratitude must rise up from the very depths of your being, it must be simple, sweet, pure white, that is, without stain; it must be free from all corruption or impurity. It is fitting, too, that this milk should be abundant, yet keeping its measure of moderation. Mark that there are several doves to be bathed and so it is necessary to have a large quantity of milk which can be poured out over each one singly. What can be better, worthier or more appropriate to the author of all grace and the most open-handed of givers than generous thanksgiving incessantly streaming forth from every virtue which you can bring into play?

The Holy Spirit comes down from heaven to visit you, and at each single coming you must pour back to him, not a single benediction, but benedictions without number. If you long to have him come again, bless him more frequently. Long ago, Isaac blessed his son, who is Christ: 'May whoever blesses you, be filled with blessings.'* To bless the Lord is, then, to plant the seeds of blessings, or to lend blessings to the Lord at interest! Indeed, from one little grain of blessing, you will carry away from the Holy Spirit many

Gn 27:29

sheaves of blessings, and a handful of seed will bring into your barns the harvest of a rich field. If you would have your barns filled with your plenty, then fill your mouth with
Cf. Ps 71:8 praise.* From the abundance of your heart
Cf. Mt 12:24 let your lips break out into a hymn.*

Far from you and from all of us be that terrible curse: 'Give them, Lord, a womb
Ho 9:14 without children and breasts without milk.'* What is a womb without children if not the gift of understanding that does not bring to birth the fruit of charity? And what are breasts without milk if not blessing and praise which lack the sweetness of devotion? God does not stop for any greeting on the way; even if anyone greets him in this way, he will not easily return the salutation. 'The soul that gives a blessing,' says Solomon, 'will be
Pr 11:23 enriched.'* True enough, but only if the blessing he gives is a rich blessing. So if you want to reap a rich harvest of blessings, do not sow them sparingly! If you want to be enriched, take pains on your side to see that
Ps 20:3 'the holocaust you offer us is a rich one!' And finally, if you want to be made drunk with gladness, you must also remember to offer the cup of joy! For so the line runs: 'The soul that gives a blessing will be enriched, and he who makes drunk with joy, will himself be
Pr 11:15 made drunk.'*

Among the pledges the spouse makes in answer to the bride, I hear this said: 'Your
Sg 7:8 breasts are like clusters on the vine.'* From vine clusters and from breasts, when either is firmly and carefully pressed, there is drawn out the wine of gladness 'which rejoices

God and man.'* The wine is pressed out into *Jg 9:13*
a cup, offered first to one and then to the other, passing now from the mouth of God to the mouth of man, now from the mouth of man to the mouth of God. Surely there is foreknowledge that this wine will make him drunk with joy, when it is said: 'My lips will rejoice when I shall sing to you'.* Surely *Ps 71:23*
there is an understanding that both share mutually in this inebriation, when it is said: 'May my words be pleasing' to you, 'for I truly delight in the Lord'?* *Ps 104:34*

You have two breasts so that in bad times as well as in good you may possess a rich flow of this kind of milk. At all times a friend gives love, so how much more does the bride of the Lord or she who in this present life longs most eagerly after the glorious name, bride? Otherwise, as Solomon says, how miserable your state if you lose your cloak on a frosty day, just when you have the greatest need of it,* and how miserable your *Cf. Pr 25:20*
state if your breasts dry up just when the praise of God is especially joyous and fitting! He who 'has given songs in the night,'* *Jb 35:10*
obviously takes pleasure in nocturnal hymns and canticles, and a song at night is sweeter in his ears than other songs. So if you want to show that your soul is truly the beloved of Jesus or is truly a mother, 'arise at night at the beginning of your time for keeping vigil!'* I go further: even when the burden of *Lm 2:19*
weakness and misfortune bears down upon you with the heaviest weight imaginable, rise up at midnight and glory in the Lord, because the Lord is good and his mercy

Cf. Ps 138:8 endures forever!* See that you do not set about it in a half-hearted way, for you bear the image of a great reality.

9. Without any doubt you are washing the eyes of Jesus, the laver of the Holy Spirit is in your hand. I speak of the laver of the Holy Spirit, with which, in a wonderful and indescribable fashion, he not only washes but is himself washed. Is his purpose to sanctify or to give delight? It seems to me to be both. For he from whom all sanctity comes, sanctifies himself in us by our ministry whenever, full of faith, with a pure conscience and secretly withholding nothing, we carry back to him whatever grace he has freely given us.

But our whole endeavor is to appear before him not only as faithful but as holy men. Let us try, as is only fitting, to make him a return in the same measure, especially the measure

Cf. Mt 7:11 of charity, which he measured out to us.* He has poured himself out upon us, and so we, in our turn, must desire most earnestly to pour ourselves out upon him. This laver that we pour out I do not hesitate to describe as a laver of delight and intense pleasure.

From this you can see, brothers, how holy and how delightful is the occupation to which you devote yourself day and night. But there are some who come insincerely and lazily, who take their hands out of this laver of the Holy Spirit to hide them behind their backs. There are some who put in a yawning and drowsy appearance at the service which the very angels must revere, the whole of which work is, in fact, accomplished in the presence and with the cooperation of the angels. Can we doubt that in the time of harvest 'poverty will come upon them like a vagabond and want like an armed man?'* For, 'it is the man who sows in blessings who will reap in blessings.'*

Pr 6:11

2 Co 9:6

It is a struggle to squeeze a little milk from our breasts, and it is with great pains that we draw it up from our hearts and breasts to make this laver for the Holy Spirit. But in exchange, he himself will soon become for us a font of milk, welling up to life eternal!* For the Spirit of God is good to anyone who in his place of exile gave service, and will lead him into a level country, into a country good and broad and flowing richly with this kind of milk.*

Cf. Jn 4:14

Cf. Ps 143:10

10. For here at last, there are the full flowing streams, brimming over with indescribable fullness, as if with the inexpressible sweetness of this milk. Here the mountains drip with sweetness, and the hills, as it is written, flow with milk and honey.* Oh my brothers, their work and ours is exactly the same kind, yet as far as concerns delight and happiness, we must sorrowfully confess that the difference between them is as great 'as the sky is lifted up above the earth!'* Meanwhile, by the grace of the Holy Spirit, we rejoice to be in some sense at rest near full flowing streams. The choir of heaven is rich and full, every throat and mouth wide-open, singing to the ears of God with jubilant sweetness, with lovely harmony, with soaring note and tireless strength. We add to it our low, hoarse and untrained voices, making a sadly raucous clamor, and yet it is the Holy Spirit within

Cf. Jl 3:18

Is 55:9

our hearts who gives us the courage. We break into a great shout of exultation: 'Praise the Lord from heaven, praise him in the
Ps 148:1 heights!'* This is how we encourage them, as if urging them on to an action exactly the same as our own. From our own choir we turn our gaze to theirs, as if to show that what we have in hand is identical. And yet, we are exiles and they are citizens, they are full flowing, we ooze drop by drop, they represent plenty and we poverty—what is there in common?

There is at least this in common, that here in this present life we enjoy the not inconsiderable consolation of having the Holy Spirit rest in the place of our exile. Granted that our enjoyment falls far short of true fruition, nevertheless his resting place is beside full-flowing streams, as we have said before, because of the likeness of our work and our joy to theirs. He is 'at rest', then, but only because, by his gift, we are at rest, waiting, contemplating, marveling, longing for those full-flowing streams from heaven.
Cf. Heb 10:23 God is faithful in his promises.* Jesus will not relax until he has fulfilled the promise
Cf. Jn 7:37 he made on the day of the great festival.* If only now could be that great feast day and Jesus deign to proclaim it to our hearts as he appears in all his splendor!

11. May it come soon, Lord Jesus, may that great day of your eternal festival come soon! Then it will be done to us according
Cf. Lk 1:38 to your word* and out of our hearts will flow
Cf. Jn 7:38 streams of living waters,* full-flowing streams to which nothing can be added. In the

meantime, may it never befall us that anything at all should draw us away from resting on their banks, until the day comes when you yourself as a river of peace stream down upon us.* You will cause many rivers to flow *Cf. Is 66:12*

into us and from us,
you who live and
reign, with God
the Father and
the Holy Spirit
one God, for
ever and
ever.
Amen.

SERMON TWENTY

The beginning of the twentieth sermon. Of the scent of the garments of the Lord Jesus, where mention is also made of Esau's garments, in which Jesus deigned to be clad. What are the cheeks of the spouse, what the cheeks of the bride, and what our cheeks; and who are the perfumers by whom the beds of spices are sown.

Sg 5:13

'HIS CHEEKS are beds of spices, sown by perfumiers.'* After a long, loving look at her beloved's eyes, the bride moves on to the feature nearest them, his cheeks. She is a woman immersed in joy, passing with a very swift and joyous movement from one source of joy to another. Here is the immense happiness of having found very many mansions in her beloved,* and she walks blissfully from one place to the next, wherever 'her pleasure inclines her,'* or rather, as the Spirit of her beloved draws her. Long ago, a column of fire and dense cloud went before the sons of Israel and if they found there, 'in a dry and pathless land without water',* many mansions, how much more shall the bride of the Lord, who has crossed the Jordan and surely entered the promised land, led on by the Spirit of her spouse? In her beloved she enters into, as it were, as

Cf. Jn 14:2

Virgil, Eclogue 2, *l. 65.*

Ps 63:1

many castles and cities as the ways and kinds of delighting which she rejoices to have found in him. So from a region of light, from contemplating the eyes of Jesus, into what might be called a region of scent, into the gardens of spices, she is led by the spirit of her spouse, and she leads her maidens after her.

2. 'His cheeks,' she says, 'are as beds of spices, sown by perfumers fragrance.'* Once in the past someone smelled the odor of sweetness coming from Jesus, and he broke forth into recollection of the richness of that sweetness.* 'See,' he said, 'the odor of my son is like the odor of a rich field.'* It is true that he was acting, as yet, at a great distance away, and from that distance he was blessing a son who would be present after many ages to come. Yet he was deeply and sweetly aware of the beauty of his odor and reached out after him with blessings. He felt for him a father's love and set upon his head glory and great splendor.*

Sg 5:13

Cf. Ps 145:5

Gn 27:27

Cf. Ps 21:5

Think about, ponder deeply, the wonderful scent the bride must drink in from the cheeks of her beloved, seeing that the scent of his garments blew so sweetly to Isaac's nostrils. Then you will understand this, that, when Isaac experienced the fragrance of his garments, he drank deep of the spirit of understanding and broke forth into cries of prayerful blessings. This is only to be expected. As it is written: 'The scent of myrrh and aloes and cassia waft from his clothes, and his ivory palaces; because of these the daughters of kings make him glad and do him honor.'* O the perfume of these garments of the Lord

Ps 45:8

Jesus! Their fragrance is so utterly indescribable, reaching and filling the nostrils not only of Isaac but even of David, that from their fragrant utterances some portion of that lovely odor has been sensed wafting to our nostrils, too.

But what are we saying? Surely these were Esau's garments, and a little while earlier they were said to be stored away at home by the hands of Rebecca? Then do we believe that Jesus' scent has breathed forth from Esau's garments? Obviously this is so.

3. Esau's garments were the desire of his father's blessing, the feeling of penitence over foolishly losing the rights of the first-born and also brotherly love which, though so recently wounded, covered with a fraternal kiss so deep a wound. Another garment was brotherly love, which a short time before had been so grievously wounded in him and at last covered the scar of the gaping wound with an affectionate embrace. So the faith of the nations and their repentance and charity even then gave forth the scent of Esau in those garments. You deigned to put on these garments, Lord Jesus, from your very cradle, and as the life-giving perfume of your cheeks breathed to the ends of the earth, the first fruits of the nations hurried to you, not forgetting to bring their gifts of spices. At that time these garments were very small, but they fitted you well enough because you were yourself very small then.

You grew in size, Lord my God, and you became very great indeed. Your greatness demanded fit attire, and so you clothed yourself in a congruous robe of many colors. You dressed yourself indeed with magnificence, but you made your dress magnificent beyond comparison by the very wearing of it. These clothes of Esau then which you deigned to put on, God of Jacob our protector,* are the fulness of the nations, taken up into your body through faith and repentance: through your most kind and varied wisdom they were changed and transfigured by the wondrous providence of the newness of the heavenly man, which you are, into a new odor and a fresh beauty.

Cf. Ps 46:3,7,11

Even your eternal wisdom itself is a mother to you, according to the dispensation whereby for our sake you took on our humanity, a mother prudent in counseling, faithful in guarding her trust, diligent in service, circumspect in making suggestions, but quick to offer help. By your mediation, she is the mother of us all and she marvelously unites us to you and you to us. All this has come about because your heavenly Father has blessed you and your blessing has been poured out from you and in you, into us as well.

It was with wisdom that these garments were stored once, hidden in her secret chamber, in the treasure house of her charity, and there they are very good indeed, when we are pleasing to her in the truth which you embody. They are indeed very good because you, who are exceedingly good on account of your admirable goodness, they fit both well and closely. From you they draw their goodness, their beauty and their fragrance so that your Father, rightly delighting in all these things, has bestowed every heavenly benediction on you in us and on us in you.

Not only the patriarchs and prophets but the very angelic powers themselves gaze in wonder at the rare novelty of this amazing deed, and they cry aloud: 'Who is this coming from Edom, in dyed garments from Bozrah, he that is glorious in his apparel,
Is 63:1 marching in the greatness of his strength?'* For to the eyes of the blessed spirits it is exceedingly strange and wonderful that he, who came down from heaven to come into Edom and dwell with Edom, and to put on the robes of Edom, and then to bear into heaven those same robes dyed with his precious blood and show them to the eyes of his Father, should deign to spread them out for the angels to behold and praise. Isaac does well to attribute the fragrance of the garments not to the garments in themselves, but to his son. 'See,' he says, 'the odor of my
Gn 27:27 son is as the odor of a rich field.'* It is the same with the angels, marveling less at the beauty of the apparel than at the glorious
Cf. Is 63:1 one who wears it.* You are unique among your holy ones, both for the sweetness of your odor and for the splendid beauty of your beautiful splendor. From their union with you they borrow for themselves whatever quality they show whether it be some beauty or the breathing of some fragrance.

This saying is yours, O Wisdom, who pro-
Cf. Si 24:5, antiphon for 17 December Vespers. ceeded from the mouth of the Most High*: 'I am the mother of fair love,' and you also say:
**Si 24:17-18* 'Like a vine I bore a fruit, sweet in the scent.'*

So when Mary Magdalen poured out her ointment, 'the whole house was filled with the perfume of the ointment,'* and this holds for whatever meaning we give to 'house'. We may apply it to some sinner, moved to repentance by the example of this sinful woman and encouraged to hope for forgiveness. We may take 'house' to mean the whole church of the saints, still a pilgrim church while on earth, or the church which is above and is free, Jerusalem, our mother.* The odor of such an ointment spreads out through the whole of earth and heaven, too. But that ointment breathed a fragrance not because it was poured out by those hands but rather because it was poured on him who is the odor of all sweetness and therefore straight way returned the fragrance it had received. Otherwise, ointments may breathe out whatever scented sweetness they please, but if they do not perpetually breathe out Jesus and do not draw their inspiration from him and in connection with him, hastening to distill themselves and breathe their last in his head or cheeks or feet or whole body, then it will be necessary to bring their breath to an immediate end and leave them to expire, pitifully, with dying flies.

Jn 12:3

Cf. Ga 4:26

4. I know your souls are waiting eagerly to hear what these cheeks of the spouse really are, and what name should fittingly be assigned to them. Unless you have some better opinion, it seems to me that his cheeks are his gaiety and gravity. The whole of a man's face becomes very pleasing in appearance if gravity gives it dignity and

gaiety gives it an appealing charm. Ripeness of years brings a grave stability that protects the mind against inexperience and heedlessness. On the other hand, gaiety dissolves the clouds of sadness, smoothes away the wrinkles or irritation, stops gnawing envy from inflicting its spiteful wounds or cures the bites it has already inflicted. Gravity turns most resolutely away from folly and idle trivialities, eager every moment to occupy the soul with weighty matters. It will never let the enemy see it and mock its day of rest.* But gaiety always holds a vessel of oil in her hand, and as the foes rush on in all their terror, she uses it to give her face a happy shine, and goes on her way rejoicing.* So cheeks are rightly spoken of in pairs. They are pairs forever associated together, two and are ever similar to each other, ever beholding each other, companions and attendants. In a mind well-disciplined, they never suffer a moment's separation.

Cf. Lm 1:7

Cf. Ac 5:41

5. But my wretched cheeks are deplorably different, either disgraced by foolish and irresponsible mirth or shrouded in gloomy severity. The scales of restraint hang equally balanced, and for me, finding that balance is extremely difficult and keeping it more difficult still. 'Unhappy man that I am!'* There have been so many cycles of the year, so many instructions in virtue, so many laws to train me, so many examples of holy gravity, all showing me forth as difficult to teach, all leaving me intractable. I am shamed to mention my cheeks, rightly so called for I have two, two little ones, for either they are

Rm 7:24

are relaxed in some unfitting levity,* or cast down by sorrow, the kind of sorrow which can expect no return except greater sadness.* Eph 5:4 Cf. RB 27:3

I lift up my eyes to the venerable gravity of those ancient patriarchs whose faces were full of gladness yet 'the light of their face did not fall to the earth'.* They shame me. I hear any one of them thundering forth in tones of terror when his brother gives way to laughter: 'In the presence of heaven and earth,' he says, 'we are about to render our account to God, and you laugh?' I once also heard another voice, not dissimilar, loud in its thunder, and my whole being trembled. The words came from a holy and truly wise man who was preparing like one of those perfumers in his garden to sow some priestly cheeks. Breaking the ground with his hoe and digging deep, he said, 'Idle talk among men of the world is merely idle talk; on the lips of a priest it is blasphemy.' And immediately after this he adds: 'Sometimes these things must be endured, but they should never be repeated.'* Jb 29:24

*Bernard, Csi 2.13.22; SBOp 3:429; CF 37:76

Then there is this, too, to consider, that in our own household we have a gardener to take care of these things. I am referring to Saint Benedict. For so many years now he has been toiling in the little garden-patch of my soul, and as well as he can, he has surrounded it with a wall, divided it into plots and sown it with scented herbs. To this very day he is waiting patiently, but, I am sadly afraid, waiting in vain to gather small bundles of fragrance from my cheeks. In their place, I fear, the time of harvest will discover thorns and nettles, the things that usually grow in the field of a lazy man.

Alas, how often this perfumer of mine, trying to renew the surface of my cheeks rises threateningly against me. He accuses me and instructs me, speaks to me and makes announcements, condemns in every place throughout the monastery all buffoonery and
RB 6:8 outbursts of laughter,* does not permit me to open my lips to them. What answer shall I make to this perfumer as he extends his pruning knife, as he opens out his hand and spreads wide the fold of his cloak? What am I to say, especially, when he begins to call as witness against me the very frequent warnings he has given me and the very profession of my vows? It was my own mouth that once pronounced these vows, and I called God and his saints to be my witness.

I have recounted all this in the first person, dearest brethren, not so much by way of example, as if wishing to warn you, but more to accuse my own self in your presence. And yet, in reality, it is doubly by way of example because I am working towards both ends, to accuse myself and, at the same time, to give you a salutary lesson. You yourselves are truly the cheeks of the Lord Jesus, his beds of spices, sown by perfumers, unless, forebear the thought, perfumers have up to now worked in you to no purpose! They have taught you goodness and knowledge with
Cf. Ps 119:66 such zeal* that now your soul refuses to be
Cf. Ps 77:2 comforted by anyone except Jesus* and, no less, it refuses to be made desolate by anyone except him either.

6. As soon as the Word of God has kissed her, the bride seems to make progress in the beauty of her cheeks, while charity is just beginning to take root in her. Among the first words honoring her with praise, she hears with deep happiness from the lips of her spouse that: 'Your cheeks are as lovely as the turtle-dove's.'* Surely, through the power of her *Sg 1:9* spouse, the bride has made her cheeks like those of the dove, in that the absence of her spouse leaves her wretched beyond all solacing, sick beyond all healing, straitened beyond all ease of movement, poor beyond all wealth, insensible to every joy there is? But when her spouse is at her side, she learns to let nothing trouble her and to stand firm against all injustice, with a quiet heart and a cheerful gravity. She sees to it that her beloved is always in her sight,* she ponders constantly *Cf. Ps 16:8* upon his face, she esteems everything else as nothing in comparison with her longing love for him. So she is very like the turtledove in its purity. She maintains inviolable her loyalty to her spouse and to him alone. She clings faithfully to him when he is with her and she sighs after him with still greater faithfulness when he is away. While he is alive she is determined to live at least for him, but when he is dead, she passes the remainder of her life in a daily funeral in ceaseless mourning.

Dearly beloved let us imitate the cheeks of this purest of doves; let us not taint the perfume or dishonor the beauty of these cheeks consecrated to our heavenly spouse with the stench and filth of useless consolations, that is if we wish to be pleasing in his

eyes, and to give forth the fragrance of spice beds in his nostrils. No human strength has an attraction powerful enough to draw us to this imitation, but who can doubt that the odor and the loveliness of his own cheeks are strong enough to draw us after him? Longing for him with all her soul, the bride says: 'Draw me after you; we will run in the odor
Sg 1:3 of your ointments'* especially since the cheeks of those who run in his pursuit are fragrant with scent, breathing in ever more plentifully the spirit of life.

7. Therefore, O Jesus my Lord, O honey-sweetness, O scented delight, O font of all that is sweet, draw me in the odor of your cheeks! With their rich beauty and perfume cleanse from our cheeks what is unclean, blow away what is fetid. Teach us at every hour to fix our whole thought on your cheeks and borrow from them some fair semblance for our own cheeks.

According to what we have received from your perfumers, I mean the prophets and evangelists, we hear reverently that in your unspeakable kindness and gentleness, for the sake of reconciling us sinners to God, your Father, you gave them to others to be
Cf. Is 50:6 plucked.* That was a very great day, the day of your Father's harvest, when he gathered to himself bundles of spices from the beds of spices which are your cheeks. With those bundles he filled his lap, there to remain stored with him for all eternity. That most delicate of perfumes breathed forth its scent as if to him alone, because 'no one knows the
Mt 11:27 Son except the Father.'*

On that day, too, the bride of Christ, the church of God, gathered her harvest of first-fruits from the beds of your cheeks, and from that day until the end of time she never ceases to reap an ever-fresh harvest from that scented seed. As is only fitting, she stores it away between her breasts. Even the synagogue had a part to play in advancing this work of love, though with evil intention and sinful deed. It compressed and squeezed tight those most sacred spices. Yet this sacrilegious boldness only made them give out perfume more freely. For the more it shamelessly struck at the cheeks of Jesus, eager to pluck and spit on them, the more they continued with even greater power and glory to breathe out into eternity the lifegiving scent of their sweetness.

Those who harvested these beds were not those who sowed them.* They were sowed by prophets, who spoke at length of the holiness and meekness of the Lord Jesus, as if in the fullest and most brilliant light of the gospel. In the gospel the Church has, for the most part, gathered nothing more than their hand sowed in their prophecies. Let me for a moment pluck a little from that most fruitful harvest—a very little, scarcely anything—and let me hold it to your nostrils to sniff its scent. What could be clearer in meaning or sweeter in smell than those words of Isaiah to which I referred a little while ago? 'I gave my body to the strikers and my cheeks to those who plucked them; I did not turn my face away from those who mocked and spat upon me.'* Other beds of that holy seed have been likewise sowed by the other prophets,

Cf. Jn 4:37

Is 50:6

all in the same spirit, all thickly planted. It is
Cf. Jn 4:38 into their labors that the Church has entered,* brought there by the loving gardener. And so that we may smell more distinctly something of the gentleness of Jesus in his suffering and the innocence of his heart absolute in its submission, he went on to say: 'He will not
Is 42:4 mourn or be disturbed,'* he will not cry out or contend, but he was silent as a lamb before
Cf. Is 53:7 his shearers and he did not open his mouth.*

Let anyone with nostrils to smell with come near! Let him gather for himself and carefully press between his fingers that bundle of spices! Let him breathe in from them the odor of every kind of gravity and serenity! Then like the careful bride of the Lord, let
Cf. Sg 1:12 him store his bundle between his breasts,* so always to have close at hand a reminder of his sweetness, especially when a time of temptation assails, when his gravity and cheerfulness in good times as well as bad is destined to be put to the test.

So, Lord Jesus, 'be our strong arm in the morning, and our protection in time of
Is 33:2 trial,'* perfuming us on every side and breathing sweetness by day and night. From the scent of your cheeks may there flow to us at all times and on each side the certainty of salvation and a continual source of healing, you who with God the Father and the Holy Spirit live and reign, God, for ever and ever. Amen.

SERMON TWENTY-ONE

The beginning of the twenty first sermon. What are the lips of Moses and what are the lips of the spouse. What is the myrrh that his lips distill, and why it is only the first myrrh they are said to distill. Also, why the myrrh is said to be distilled and not rather poured out.

'HIS LIPS DISTILL the purest myrrh.'* *Sg 5:13* 'Lord, open my lips,'* that I may *Ps 51:15* declare the praise of those lips of yours, perhaps not fully or worthily, but still, very lovingly. Let my Lord be the first to speak, so that my reply may not be out of place. Let him distill into my heart some of the secret sweetness of his honeyed lips, which will also be like sweet honey in my mouth* *Cf. Ezek 3:3* so that I shall not be ashamed to speak to him face to face, seeing that he has first opened his lips to his servant.

But what are my lips, Lord Jesus, in comparison with those sacred lips of yours? You are the true high priest, and I confess to you that 'I am a man of unclean lips'.* *Is 6:5* They can only be cleansed if in some way they receive your touch. But you are also the true and highest seraph, not only inflaming your servants, but making them a flaming fire.* *Cf. Ps 104:4* I beseech you, bring me a coal of fire from the altar of your love,* *Cf. Is 6:6* to make my lips holy and pure, to make them burn with a living flame. Your bride was set on fire by coals like these, borne to her by the hand of her spouse, and that spouse is yourself. For all who love you, she has herself become a living coal. She takes you, her beloved, wholly into her hands, and depicts you to us in different images and figures, displaying to our minds your head, your hair, your eyes, cheeks, lips, and all the other lovely features of your beauty. She does not show them as they really are, nor even as she has merited to understand them, but as much as befits our earthly state of 'maidenhood', presuming that she thinks us deserving of the graces that go with being a maiden.

2. Yet, when I consider what is said in praise of your lips, I must admit I am disturbed that it is myrrh that they distill. Myrrh is pungent indeed, but it is bitter. Why not rather honey or the honeycomb or something similar, delicious as nectar and of piercing sweetness? Then there would be a double pleasure, delicious to taste while also lovely to smell. Consequently, if myrrh is to stand for some grace, what does it mean when it says that the first myrrh distills from the lips of the spouse? For it stands without question that myrrh is the first to drip from those lips, for it is clear that not only the first and second but every grace flows therefrom. For the Wisdom of God, which you are, says: 'In me is all grace of the way and of truth, in me is
Sir 24:25 all hope of life and of virtue.'*

Finally, it is no less troubling to find this myrrh distilled and not rather poured out. To speak of pouring out would throw into much higher relief the glory of this most generous and munificent of spouses, who himself says in another context, 'I shall pour out my spirit upon all flesh'.* Falling in droplets betrays the parsimony of want and poverty. And so when David was once inspired to song by the loveliness of the fairest of the children of men, and took up his pen to sing his deeds to the king, he began his song by praising his lips. He burst forth without premeditation, 'Grace is poured forth in your lips, therefore God has blessed you for ever more'.* I am surely not wrong in thinking it is by the same Spirit that David and the bride of Christ abandon themselves freely in their bridal hymns to a whole-hearted praise of their same spouse. What she calls myrrh, he describes as grace, and what one calls the first, the other speaks of as if in some way being the cause of other graces. 'Therefore,' he says, 'God has blessed you for ever more.'*

Joel 2:28

Ps 45:3

Ibid.

Grace was indeed poured on those lips at the moment when the Father greeted him with the blessing of all sweetness and anointed him with the fulness of his spirit, so that not even the hem of his garment was without a touch of this most generous anointing.* 'But if anyone does not have the Spirit of Christ, he does not belong to him.'* So because he received completely and beyond measure, according to the wisdom given him by the Father, he shared with us a measure of what had been accorded him. For him, there is an outpouring, for us, there is a distilling. His lot is to have the fulness, those who share with him, to have a share. Both are rejoicing

Cf. Ps 133:2

Rom 8:9

in the same free flowing fountain of blessing, but through his lips, as if through a channel, the flow is drawn off to those he associates with himself. For to those living waters, above the heavens, there is no way for us to approach, nor for them to us, except through him. 'At the coming of the God of Sinai, at the coming of the God of Israel, the heavens', he says, 'distilled' a generous rain,* which God set apart for his inheritance.* For my part, I cannot believe any heavens could be more lofty or more brilliant than the lips of Jesus.

Ps 68:8
Cf. Ps 68:9

3. But what precisely are these lips of Jesus? Here let that disciple 'whom Jesus loved, who rested on the breast of Jesus at the supper,'* let him reply for me. This is what he says, 'The law was given through Moses, grace and truth came through Jesus Christ'.* The lips of Moses are the rigor of harshness, the shadow of the truth. For we have the witness of the apostle that the work of the law is only wrath;* it showed the disease but offered no remedy, rather despairing at its own weakness and impotence and leaving its patient dead. It issued stern commands, and laid impossible burdens on men's shoulders. If at times they fell beneath the weight, it stretched out no hand in support, did not even touch them with its finger.* With a worthless and transitory promise and under a sort of coarse veil of symbol, it did not so much raise souls up to heaven as set them down on the earth. She who was once your bride, O Moses, (I am speaking of the synagogue) was wounded rather than healed by the array of cruel

Jn 21:20
Jn 1:17
Rom 4:15
Cf. Mt 23:4

remedies you offered her. She had every reason to say, 'You are to me a spouse of blood'.* *Ex 4:25*

4. How sweet your spouse, O bride, in comparison, how lovable, how mighty! Not with sword and stone, not even with scourge and rod, but with grace poured out on his lips, distilling from his lips as he desires, he heals all your sickness both effectually and gently.* *Cf. Ps 45:3* You have indeed every reason to say to him, 'You are to me a spouse of grace. Freely you have given me faith, holy fear, remission of my sins, this awareness of your love which sets my heart aglow. Freely you will one day give me, I am confident, the very happiness of life eternal, and that is clearly nothing else than to love you totally and cleave to you for ever.

But you are also to me, not indeed a spouse of blood, but a spouse in blood. I was redeemed by your blood, washed in your blood, given your blood to drink and by it made mystically drunk. Through it I hold within my heart the surest pledge of eternal restoration. The blood of my spouse is both the price of my redemption and the laver of my purification; it is the cup that sustains my exile and at the same time a strong incentive to my love, being, as it is, such clear proof of his love. And finally, I whisper into my spouse's ear,* *Antiphon for the Feast of St Agnes (21 January)* his blood adorns my cheek. With its strong flood of rich color, it blots out all the old blackness, conveying something of its own beauty to an Ethiopian servant girl.* *Cf. Sg 1:5* So then he need not be ashamed to call me his beloved, and I likewise, can dare to speak of him as mine.

5. But now, let us come back to the lips of the spouse. We have called them 'grace and truth',* and from both these qualities salvation certainly flows in abundance. Grace is like a healing balm easing the wounds of the sick, and truth is like the wine of contrition, probing the depths of those wounds. The one has a gentle sweetness, the other a health-giving bite. Therefore the grace of salvation from the lips of Jesus, a grace, that is, distilling grace and truth, is quite clearly myrrh, for it is perfumed through its sweetness and bitter through its truth.

Cf. Jn 1:16

To the sick soul, truth is very bitter, and to eyes that are still weak, light is painful. Yet when love is already awakening into life through the unction of the Spirit, the eyes begin to see clearly, and the absence of the light of truth is most keenly felt. If it is not present, it is ardently pursued. So is it here. This myrrh of the beloved may hold bitterness, but the bride loves what comes from his lips, whatever it is; she drains it thirstily, guards it joyfully. She is very conscious of the body, which, as the apostle says, 'is dead on account of sin',* and therefore subject to a twofold law, that of sin and death, and she is equally conscious that this myrrh brings the healing of a twofold incorruptibility. For, in the words of the apostle, the law of the Spirit of life, which is no other than the grace distilling from the lips of Jesus, has freed me from the twofold law of sin and death.* Though I am a wretched man and pitiable slave, compelled by inescapable necessity

Rom 8:10

Cf. Rom 8:2

to serve both these laws, yet this first myrrh flowing from those saving lips has released me from his servitude. At the unction of this myrrh, the poisonous corruption teeming vilely in soul as in body, suddenly subsides. The worm that never dies but always grows again from both, from this moment on begins to sicken, and is obviously marked out for eventual death, provided that, as before, this myrrh keeps on gently flowing drop by drop. And so my flesh, though foul and corrupt and nothing else in itself than the destined fodder of death and the worms that live for ever, has nevertheless drawn into itself, from the Spirit of Jesus, the fresh, unmistakable scent of life and incorruption. As the apostle says, 'If the Spirit of God dwells within us, he who raised Jesus from the dead will also bring our mortal bodies to life, through the Spirit dwelling within us.'* How much more, then, by the same grace, will our soul enter fully into the joy of his freedom and incorruptibility? For even our flesh, so closely and completely united to the soul, sharing in its fulness, is one day to share also in this anointing.

Rom 8:11

6. How good this myrrh is! Not only does it protect the body from death's corruption, but it defends both outer and inner man from eternal death. It restores the outer man to life, it anoints the inner man for the resurrection. This is why my heart and my flesh exult with equal joy in the living God.* While the heart is already reaping the happiness of its resurrection, the flesh too has the privilege of tasting in advance some of the firstfruits of its resurrection. It is like one before a rich

Cf. Ps 84:2

harvest in all the gladness of hope and the
Cf. Jn 7:6 fullness of the time of his writing.* Hence that cry of exultation leaping up from the tents of the penitent, 'My flesh has bloomed again, and I will thank him with all my
Ps 28:7 heart'.* And again, 'Therefore my heart is glad and my tongue rejoices, and even my
Ps 16:10 flesh shall rest in confidence'.*

The reason, I think, why such healing and life-giving myrrh is described as first, is to avoid any suspicion that the beloved may have kept one kind for himself and shared another with his own. The bride has seen to it that the pettiness of such a suggestion is kept at a great distance from the generosity of her spouse, for she can only judge of him
Cf. Wis 1:1 with a great and noble heart.* So she says of the myrrh that distills from his lips that it is not just of any kind, but the first, in other words, the very same kind with which he himself was anointed. There is of course, this difference, that he was anointed both interiorly and exteriorly, and from this completeness of anointing he alone is truly called Christ, the Anointed One. Yet, as the apostle says, 'he who sanctifies and those who are
Heb 2:11 sanctified have all one origin,'* and there is obviously only one Spirit of Anointing, by which the Father anointed his only begotten, and he anointed his bride.

7. But the Son possesses a triple privilege which sets him far above all those who share with him in this anointing. From the very first moment of his conception in the virgin's womb, he was anointed. He was conceived through the Holy Spirit, and, above all

measure, every last drop of unction was poured out upon him. So much so, that from him and by him, the overflowing abundance of this anointing streamed down upon the hem of his garment, which is the church.* First, then, he was anointed before all others, and second, above all others, and third, for the sake of all others, not just for himself alone. *Cf. Ps 133:2*

Those who share in this unction, have grace poured into their hearts, for he distills it, but this does not mean they also have it on their lips. They are enabled to receive into themselves the grace that comes from heaven, and this in itself is without any doubt a sufficiently divine favor. With great truth John could assert, that 'no one can receive anything unless it is given to him from heaven'.* Yet really to produce it in others, in just the same extent as they have themselves received it, this is not within the scope of the grace or glory proper to men or to angels. This belongs only to him who is the only Son of the Father. *Jn 3:27*

For as that same friend of the bridegroom says, 'he who is sent from God,' only he and not another, 'he it is who speaks the words of God'.* For the words of the Creator, unutterable by his creation, are the utterance of divine inspiration. Only words like these are words of strength, only they are living and lifegiving. Only those who listen to them are alive, and whoever listens to them, although in the grave, rises immediately into life.* So whatever lifegiving spirit they breathe, *Jn 3:34* *Cf. Jn 5:28-29*

those who hear these words, if they withdraw from their ears even for a moment, then with the silence of the word, there will be deafness, and if life departs from them, then death will reign supreme. This is why, as long as I live and have the spirit of life in my nostrils, I shall not cease to cry out to you, O Lord, 'Do not be deaf to me, for if you become silent to me,' if you become silent even for a single second, I shall immediately die, and 'become like those who go down into the
Ps 28:1 pit.'* Instead, without any interruption, let my God speak to the heart of his servant, let him speak the words of God, and that means, justice and peace.

I know well who it was who said, 'I am he
Is 63:1 who speaks justice,'* he who is supremely the defender of our salvation. But also, of no one but the only Son of the Father has it been
Zech 9:10 written, 'He will speak peace to the peoples'.* O, if only I too could hear 'what my Lord
Ps 85:8 God speaks within me,'* whether he has counted me among his people or among his holy ones or finally among those 'who have
Ibid. turned to him in their hearts'.* Let him put his servant in any place and condition that seems best to him, provided only that he himself speaks in my ears and makes the 'glory
Is 30:30 of his voice be heard'* in the gladness of my heart.

With beautiful precision, therefore, the bride expresses the unique glory of her spouse by saying, 'His lips distill the purest
Sg 5:13 myrrh.'* It is as if she were to say, 'No one
Jn 7:46 has ever spoken like this man.'* For my beloved speaks not only in human language,

but as 'the only Son who is in the bosom of the Father,'* from his divine lips he distills the mysteries of God into the ear of the heart. He speaks of completely ineffable things, and in an ineffable manner. He speaks of what he has heard from his Father, and in the manner he has learnt from his Father.* And what man is fit even to think of these things?

Jn 1:18

Cf. Jn 15:15

In the lips of the beloved the bride seems to have signified the unique power and glory of his inner breathing within us, in the distilling the gentleness and wisdom of this breathing, and in the first myrrh the excellence and power of the gift he has breathed upon us. For he alone is glorious and powerful who can turn the mind of man, with the utmost speed and ease, in whatever direction he chooses; he alone is gentle and wise who knows how to do this with calm unction and wise discretion; he alone is good and humble who graciously shares his own spirit with his little ones. To him be honor, glory, power and majesty, for ever and ever.

Amen.

SERMON TWENTY-TWO

The beginning of the twenty-second sermon. That the lips of Jesus distill grace in different ways, because they can be closed or apart, pressed together or open wide. About his two kinds of silence. About the bitterness of penitence, which is what the bride means by the 'purest myrrh'. Why mention is made only of the purest myrrh, and why it is said to be distilled.

Sg 5:13 'HIS LIPS DISTILL the purest myrrh.'* Whatever those sacred lips distill, the lips, O bride, of your beloved, it has a marvelous power to make me thirsty, to make me long to drink my fill. For how long a time will your beloved, who is my Master, keep me on short commons and not permit me to drink deep of the moisture of his lips,
Cf. Job 7:19 my salvation?* I know for certain that whoever drinks that is blessed. Even if the full meaning of this myrrh is not yet present to the mind, its breath has certainly already touched my desire. Your word showers little sparks from the fire of sacred love upon us before it shines clear before our senses, and while still hidden from the eyes of our understanding, it has already wounded the heart.

2. I should like to know about the

beloved's lips, whether they distill this first myrrh when they are closed or open, tight shut or wide apart. For I remember having read that at times he held his lips in silence, and again, at other times, opened them, as he says himself, 'I will not restrain my lips, Lord, as you well know.'* This is plainly to make known some word of wisdom. When it is a question of his closing his lips tight so as to bestow a holy kiss, then the only one who can be asked is the Lord's bride. While her love was young and the sighs of her panting heart yet faint she broke into a cry, shameless perhaps, but bold, addressed not to her beloved—her confidence had not progressed so far—but to herself, perhaps with the holy angels and God as her witness: 'Let him kiss me with the kiss of his mouth!'* Then, we all know how he opened his lips wide apart after his resurrection. He showed himself to his loved ones, breathed upon them and said to them, 'Receive the Holy Spirit.'*

Ps 40:9

Sg 1:1

Jn 20:22

So, whichever of these shapes the lips of the beloved take, must we not call fragrant the drops that distill from them? There can be no doubt about it.

3. My Lord Jesus was silent before the scribes and pharisees when they accused him, silent before his judges when they questioned him, silent before those who punished him with torture and crucifixion. Even today, he is silent before the wicked and shameless men who challenge him every day and every hour. If this is so, then plainly that silence of his is full of grace and truth.*

Cf. Jn 1:14

Apparently the Stoics.

There was once a philosophy of this world* which had very strict rules of silence and believed that they would be enabled to stand undaunted amid the searching challenge of various ill-usage. So much so, that those who adhered to this system, only prided themselves on becoming philosophizers when they had finally mastered the discipline of this holding of the tongue. But there is no comparison at all between this senseless philosophy and the true wisdom, which is Christ. Whether their lips were open or closed, they were still completely dry, with no least trace of holy unction. How could they possibly distill to others when they were lacking all the richness of moisture within their own selves? They said that they were wise, because by their own reckoning they were patient, and yet they were as far banished from patience as from true wisdom. The man who wants to enter into the treasuries of wisdom has to bow his neck low at the very threshold and, according to the true philosophy of Paul, to become stupid in order to be wise.* Thin and arid lips like these could distill no myrrh, or if by some chance they did, then the myrrh was certainly not the first. The blessed testimony of a good conscience, the glorious hope of the kingdom, the sweet charity of Christ, the gentle consolation of the Paraclete —none of these either glowed in their hearts or dripped from their lips.

Cf. 1 Cor 3:18

4. But the true tree of this myrrh is the fruitful silence of Jesus. It drew its patience from the true fount of wisdom, unknown to the wise of this world, and it said to the

Father, 'For you, O Lord, are my patience.'* *Ps 71:5*
And again: 'Lord God, you are my helper, and so I am not put to shame, so I have set my face like a flint.'* The patience of Jesus *Is 50:7*
is a flint, flint-hard, and yet anointed with the oil of gladness, and so very gentle.

Which of you, dearest brothers, will give his heart to being a loving imitator of this sacred silence? Who will enter that school of hidden philosophy, and sit at Jesus' feet? Who will fix his whole attention on Jesus' mouth and catch the drops of myrrh distilling from it to water the earth?* And at the sight of *Cf. Ps 72:6*
Jesus keeping his peace in such tranquility, who of you is willing to put his finger to his own mouth, to rank himself with those kings whom admiration at his virtue and a generous desire to imitate it, induced to close their own mouths because of him?* *Cf. Is 52:15*

That silence of his is a living and effectual word,* and it is those 'who have ears to hear', *Cf. Heb 4:12*
who hear it.* Utterly remote from that *Mt 11:15*
silence are murmuring and complaint, remote are gnawing grief, the constriction of fear and jealous rage, remote are threats and reproaches; from those most pure, most loving and most tender lips, everything of this nature is utterly remote. 'The mouth of the just man,' says Solomon, 'has brought forth wisdom.'* Would you like to know what the *Pr 10:31*
mouth of this just man brought forth by keeping silence, and what the fruit was of that bringing forth? The hands which men had stretched out on the cross, he stretched out to his Father, and from the infinite riches of his patience he cried out this word of love:

'Father,' he said, 'forgive them, for they know
Lk 23:34 not what they do.'* Here indeed we have the purest myrrh, containing in its sense of pain no little bitterness, but in its dutiful striving much fragrance and healing.

5. For your part, then if you truly believe that you have enrolled in this school, you will not consider that you have yet become a philosopher, in the full sense of the word, if your lips refrain from speech when a brother insults you, but the depths of your heart swell with anger over the quarrel. It is not enough for the tongue to maintain a strict silence outwardly, while all the time fury rages within. Make it your ambition, according to the words of the sage, that your lips
Cf. Pr 10:32 consider what is pleasing.* By earnest prayer and a gentle reply, both in words and in kindly action, strive to win the victory, first over your own spirit, and then over the spirit of the one who injures you. Try to lead them both together as captives into the kingdom of meekness. Listen to wisdom itself, drawing you to apply yourself to this kind of philosophy, 'Seek wisdom, my son, and rejoice my heart, so that you may be able to make a
Pr 27:11 reply when you are reproached.'* And in case an evil interpretation should twist the meaning of reply into the sense of a malicious answer, it says again, 'A soft answer turns
Pr 15:1 away wrath.'* But the man who learns to answer like this, is not defrauded of his rightful reward. He is given this promise, 'He who replies in the right way will be kissed on the
Pr 24:26 lips.'*

'The right way' must be carefully studied,

and it needs real application and great help from God. It entails a virtuous silence amidst quarrels, speaking only to restore peace, and offering kindness in exchange. O, if 'you would let your mercy come to me, Lord, your salvation according to your word!'* Then I, *Ps 119:41* too, should answer for those who taunt me,* but it will be the kind of answer that *Cf. Ps 119:42* enables me to rejoice my mother's heart, and you are that mother. It will enable me to win the favor of receiving from those holy lips the great condescension of a kiss, if a sinner has any right to say such a thing.

Believe me, my brothers, the patience I am talking about is a royal anointing. It breathes out the immortal quality of goodness and kindness, and it puts to death, almost as if by an infusion of myrrh, the immortal worms. And what are these worms? Listen to the apostle, 'Let all bitterness and anger and clamor and scandal be far removed from you, with all malice.'* These are the most *Eph 4:31* deadly of worms, who draw their life from what makes us die, who nourish themselves by consuming us, and who are completely satiated by what drains us to the dregs. If the unction of this myrrh does not either smother them as they are about to be born, or, once born, does not set about wiping them all out, then there is an hereditary and everlasting law that comes into force. For the soul in which they are born, in which they have lived, on which they have fed, is to be their possession for ever. As the apostle says, 'Wrath and fury, tribulation and distress, for every human being that does evil.'* *Rom 2:8*

6. The silence of Jesus has also this quality, that it uses its myrrh to disguise the sins of those who do wrong. The souls of sinners are like foul corpses, oozing diseased and poisonous fluid, yet they are covered over with that myrrh, as if with some heavenly and living oil. For this myrrh, as indeed we know, we who have begun to come to life again from the touch of its drops, this myrrh has a real bitterness, but, more important in every way, it has a real power to save.

You have been silent to me, Lord Jesus, I grieve to think for how long, and I, intellectually heavy and dead, did not understand that the aim of your rich silence was to bring me to repentance. That life-giving liquid was falling on me from your lips, drop by drop. It was poured like a medicine through all my veins, into the very marrow of my bones where already the rottenness of concupiscence was thickly swarming, and it joyfully probed in to discover it. Even to this very day it does not cease continually to exert its healing force, until death, which had begun its reign in me, has been finally put to death!

Now I can hear with joy what I used to hear with great fear when I first began to breathe in new life. Then I was just freshly breaking out of my tomb, and you reproached me, not
Cf. Ps 6:1 in your anger but in your mercy,* and stood before me to say, 'You have done these
Ps 50:21 things, and I have been silent.'* True enough, Lord Jesus, I have indeed done these things, these and others, and all the while, you have been silent. Yet though your lips were silent,

you were silently devoting yourself to the task of my salvation. That silence of yours was strenuously active on my behalf, preparing me for eternal life and bringing it to birth in me, by the gentle way you held your peace.

It is my conviction that through that silence I received a sure answer from the Holy Spirit, and I know it from what happened. My whole flesh had become covered with corruption, because I was dead as far as you were concerned, my God. The rot had entered my bones and ravaged my very marrow, all the more destructive as it went deeper into me. Yet it seemed to me, that the first wild teeming died down to a large extent as soon as your myrrh was poured in. For it was not only my flesh that corruption laid waste, but my bones, too, and the very core of me. I had become a slave to sins, not only of the body but also of the soul, and I stumbled unceasingly from one to the other. How I bless you, Lord my God! At the sight of your face, these two kinds of death departed, and two kinds of life began to make their entry. Now I am alive, alive in body and alive in soul, able to confess that you, the Lord God, are my savior, all the days of my life!* *Cf. Is 38:20*

7. Nevertheless, though death may have departed, the shadow of death has not, nor has its sting. To this very day, 'there is no health in my flesh,' but also, 'there is no peace in my bones.'* Anything that death had *Ps 38:3* formerly seized in its grip, is now under the sway of weakness. Death inflicted a mortal wound; a remedy was applied, but health returned with dragging step and by paths

very difficult and, to me, inscrutable. Whenever I believe that I have been reformed in a certain newness of mind, and have so completely put on the new man that my heart and my flesh can rejoice in the living God,* then all of a sudden I fall back all over again into my old state of being. 'My life is cut short, as by the weaver, and while I am still beginning my web,'* I am cut off.

Cf. Ps 84:2

Is 38:12

I am weary, therefore, and in this dreary time of waiting to grow strong again, I pine away, full of self-pity. And so, after many tears, whether I want to or not, I am finally forced to knuckle under to the rules of your medicinal treatment, rules through which you skilfully devise our salvation in and from these very weaknesses themselves. Indeed, 'it is hard to kick against the goad,'* and so shall I do my best to go to meet your will, I shall await you with patience, Lord, because this is your decree, to mete out my salvation to me very gradually, as it were in drops of saving compunction.

Acts 9:5

8. Let me repeat, Lord Jesus, you fall on me drop by drop, drops tasting somewhat bitter, and yet I delight in them as in drops of morning dew. I know how utterly that dew is a dew of benediction, and how it will make my bones flourish like the grass.* I will not shrink from the bitterness which I know to be the foundation of my health. This myrrh is precious, distilling from the savior's lips to rescue us from eternal torment by the easy substitution of a momentary grief. It is a fine sort, and truly 'its price is from the far off coasts.'* Through it, all things lose their

Cf. Is 66:14

Pr 31:10

bitterness, and then again, all things appear pleasant.

Readily, then, and with glad good will, I will accept the cup of salvation from the hand of the Saviour,* especially since I read that he himself, in his passion, was given to drink of a cup where wine was mixed with myrrh.* I will drink deep of whatever draft he has prepared for me, tasting first the old wine, and hoping later that his generosity will make me taste the greater joy of the new. For by a sure and heavenly decree, 'this cup cannot pass away, unless I drink it.'*

Cf. Ps 116:13

Cf. Mk 15:23

Mt 26:42

Only this first myrrh can staunch the flow of my corruption; the excitement of physical lust can only be cleansed and made wholesome by the antidote of compunction. There is a bitterness that knows no ending, and it can only be brought to an end by the taste of bitterness itself. Oh how wretched the folly that keeps by for the morrow the dregs at the bottom of the cup, while refusing to taste the pure wine offered in this present life! Oh the unhappiness of thou threatened by the fearful prospect of being made drunk on the cup of the Lord's wrath and on the wrath of that cup! Quite certainly that most bitter of cups must be for ever drained and never drunk dry, continually swallowed down and to all eternity not exhausted nor eventually emptied. I shall taste first the wine of this cup, the first wine, the strongest, the purest. I will taste first, I say. I will drink, and as much as is good for me. I will sip it with due moderation, lest, taking it immoderately, I myself be swallowed up.*

Cf. Is 58:7

9. Since you, O Lord in your compassion, break for us the bread of tears, when we are hungry, even when we refuse it, your lips distill this first myrrh, according to our capacity. We are given to drink with the utmost prudence and love. It is not over bitter and there is not too much of it, or while pursuing the disease, it might undermine the nature, and the search for health unexpectedly end in death.

Perhaps, also, in letting us just taste of your cup, you wanted to make something clear to us. You deigned to taste—but with prudence and consideration, lest a draught too bitter and too abundant, lest in pursuing our disease, it undermine our nature and in seeking our
Cf. Mt 27:34 health it bring death upon us.* This is the factor that regulates the amount of your medicine, and with this your love has no quarrel. But whatever the size of our drink, if I look at the volume of the cup or at the load of our sickness, what we have is a mere sip, but if I turn to the severity of its bitter flavor, it is enough to make us drunk.

10. How often it happens, Lord Jesus, that I feel the castle of my soul is beset by an oppressive siege and hemmed in on all sides, on one hand the pains of death, on the other,
Cf. Ps 18:4 the pains of hell!* Then there are the torrents of iniquity, more terrible than an army in battle array, that ring me round and blockade me in and mount an attack. At the sight of so mighty a host, my soul is seized with trembling, I cannot withstand the length of the seige, and all of a sudden I hand myself over as a prisoner, caught by immeasurable

pain. I am swept off, loaded with chains, and hurled into a narrow dungeon, into the thick darkness of passionate grief. There I pass my solitary days, laying my face in the dust and 'eating ashes for my bread.'* 'I do not turn my face away' from my thoughts that 'mock and spit on me.'* Incessantly and pitilessly, my mind mulls over whatever I have done wrong since the days of my youth.

Cf. Lam 3:29

Is 50:6

In this state I have but one consolation, the very sharpness of this passionate grief of mine, and the volume and frequency of my outbursts of weeping. In giving full vent to my grief, I considerably temper the sharp acid of my cup. It is as if I make payment, as far as I can, to those who would collect my debts. So although this bitterness I find exceedingly bitter,* both within and without it works on me in the manner of an unction, distilling the sure hope of salvation, like myrrh coming from the lips of Jesus. For, after a little, 'according to the greatness of my heart's sorrow,'* that same myrrh will yield its perfume, 'like choice myrrh,'* and furnish unmistakable proof of whence it has come, and why.

Cf. Is 38:17

Ps 94:19

Cf. Sir 24:20

11. It needs no effort to explain why this kind of myrrh is described as 'the first'. The purest is the very first, what stands at the very beginning of life's journey to greet those who are setting out on it. It anticipates all the other gifts of grace, as if it were truth springing from the earth, for this very end that, justice may look down from heaven.* Truth itself, of course, is also justice, but because it takes

Cf. Ps 85:11

its rise from the earth, it has something of a bitter taste about it, whereas justice, which is from heaven, has only a sweet and scented unction, with no trace of harshness. Moreover, the eye of truth is severe, while justice, which is from heaven, has a mild and gracious countenance. This is why I think it is the former which is called by the bride the 'first myrrh', and she wants the latter to be classed second. What comes from heaven is all heavenly, possessing completely all the fragrance and incorruptibility that myrrh can offer, yet with none of its bitterness.

But if there is a myrrh which is more choice than the first myrrh, it will appear, not surprisingly, very strange that it was not rather that myrrh which the bride described as distilling from her beloved's lips. Or is it perhaps this way, that in heaven they distill one myrrh, which is from heaven, and on earth, another, which is of the earth? And then it might follow, that, compared to the heavenly myrrh, the other might be passed over as if too bitter, and so, in this present life, it must be recommended to the maidens? That would be a very wise and prudent measure. Some small taste of the drops that fall from heaven might give the maidens a distaste for the distillations of the first myrrh, and they might reject it as unnecessary, as if they were already up above. The bride is well aware how suitable the use of this myrrh is in their weakness, and how, if it ceased for one moment to distill, the corruption which a little before had gone to sleep, and the worms which up to then had slumbered, would immediately wake up again.

Alas, whenever I have gained the slightest touch with my lips of this divine sprinkling, I have become fastidious and disdain my former condition: after the smallest glimpses of a new light I shun the darkness within me. What I yearn after, I have the desire to grasp but not the strength; what I shrink from, I have the strength to hold at any time, but not the desire. Eventually, though unwilling and dejected, I turn back to my darkness, and have no desire to come out of it until the former light breaks in upon me and completely dispels it. It is in vain, my brothers, a waste of my time, for me to rise before that former light begins, or to lift up my unhappy head.* Whatever has shone on me in this present life, except that light alone, is a prison to me, and it is night, until as I sit in my darkness, that light suddenly rises upon me in all its accustomed glory and proclaims the breaching of the prison walls.

Cf. Ps 127:2

So, sitting there, this is the work and task I set myself, to catch with eagerly attentive hands the unction flowing from the lips of Jesus. From my hands and my fingers, may it distill to all my limbs, and may it zealously anoint me all over with the fire I enkindle within me. May you, too, dearest brethren, find these changes taking place more often within yourselves, since you are sons of light: this is what I hope, long and pray for. May it all come about through the very Light himself,* the Only Son of the Father, who with that the same Father and the Holy Spirit lives and reigns, God, for ever and ever. Amen.

Cf. Jn 12:36

SERMON TWENTY-THREE

The beginning of the twenty-third sermon. Of how the spouse opens his lips, and of the words of grace, virtue and wisdom that come forth from his mouth. Of the four kinds of wisdom that the true wisdom of God reveals as foolishness: the wisdom of the flesh, of the law, of the world and of the mighty.

Sg 5:13 'HIS LIPS DISTILL the purest myrrh.'* The silence of the spouse was discussed in the previous sermon, as fully as the spouse himself made possible. There remains, equally through his generosity, something to be said about how he opens his lips, how he presses them tight and how he stretches them wide apart. This will serve to praise him, and also to strengthen your faith, as well as my own. Indeed, a promise to do this was implicit in the logic of the previous section, as I know your charity has not overlooked. May that charity make you as eager to demand as I am to fulfill!

May my God keep far away from you that numbness of tooth with which he once threatened a rebellious house, speaking to them who hated his words, with a terrible curse on his mouth!* I am saying this because I do not want you to be overtaken by that grave disease of finding weariness or distaste

Cf. Ez 18:2

in listening to this marriage song. This would be as if your teeth were to be set on edge from eating sour grapes,* and so make you find bitter and acid what is quite certainly 'sweeter than honey and the honeycomb.'* *Cf. Jer 31:29* *Ps 19:10*

What is the point of fixing your gaze too intently on the rather slovenly dress of the servant who attends you, or turning in disgust from the cheapness of the vessels which convey his unworthy word? Think rather of the drink you are being offered, and from what stock grew that vine. Hear with gladness the glad words of the bride, as she comes up to you from wine cellars, 'My beloved is to me a cluster of cypress blossom, from the vineyards of Engedi.'* *Sg 1:14*

So, as was shown in the previous sermon, there is great power in the silence of Jesus. By his patience and meekness sinners are drawn to repentance and saved by the myrrh of a contrite spirit from sin's corruption and the bite of the everlasting worm. What then will it be when he opens his mouth and the grace of his lips no longer holds itself in restraint? 'Our mouth is open to you, O Corinthians,' says the apostle, and he adds the reason: 'Our heart is wide.'* We have a final witness from the mouth of Truth himself: 'The good man out of his good treasure brings forth good, and from the abundance of the heart the mouth speaks.'* *2 Cor 6:11* *Mt 12:35,34*

2. Therefore that 'good man', the only one truly good among the sons of men, the only one truly rich with boundless treasure, speaks as befits the royal grandeur of his heart and his resources. He opens his mouth

to words of grace, virtue and wisdom, words beyond the reach of any utterance of man or even angel. Only he whom God sent and who is the true Son of the true God, can speak the words of God, as John tells us in his
Cf. Jn 3:34 gospel.* No words but those of God can be addressed to what is not, and give it being, to what is created, and make it continue in being, to what is living, and make it increase
Cf. Gen 1:22 and multiply .*God is the only one who at his pleasure calls into life, and then sends to death, saying to this man, 'Come', and he comes, and to another, or rather the same
Mt 8:9 man, 'Go, and he goes.'*

Truly that man is the all powerful son of the all powerful God, who utters words not dissimilar to those of God, saying to the
Jn 11:43 dead man, 'Rise,' and he comes;* to the
Lk 18:42 blind, 'See, and immediately he sees;'* to the deaf ear, 'Open up,' and at
Cf. Mk 7:43 once it is opened;* to the man with a withered arm, 'Stretch out your arm', and he
**Mk 3:5 †Mt 8:3* stretches it;'* to the leper, 'Be clean',† and straight away he is clean; to the cripple, 'Take
Mt 9:6 up your bed,'* and he takes up his bed. He orders the sea to be still, and it is still, the winds to be quiet, and there comes a great
Cf. Mt 8:26 silence, an immense peace.* When he curses
Cf. Mt 21:19 the fig, it dries up.* When he rebukes the demons, they fall silent. When he commands, they come out, when he gives permission, they
Cf. Mk 5:13 rush into a herd of swine.*

As the centurion had the faith to realize,
Cf. Mt 8:9 this man is in all truth the Lord of armies.* Everything is a soldier in his ranks, and obeys him instantly. When the Lord draws near,

there is no slightest trace of reluctance, but an eager haste to fulfil his least command. In his armies are health and sickness, life and death, holy angels and evil devils, and he says to one, 'Go,' and he goes, and to another, 'Come,' and he comes.* Mt 8:9

Would you agree with me, I wonder, that this is the choice myrrh, flowing freely from the lips of Jesus and dispelling sickness, while it bestows life and health? Surely this myrrh is more choice than that which can do nothing more than preserve dead bodies from their collapse into disintegration?

3. Shame on you, O Jew, that such obvious power of speech has not yet revealed to you the Son of God. Name me one respect in which he shows himself either unworthy of or unlike his Father. If he does not do the works of his Father,* if what he says is lacking Cf. Jn 10:37 the divine efficacy, then, Land of Judah, you are innocent, your infidelity is not a sin, the blood of your murder cannot be held against you. But if, on the other hand, he wields power as God, and speaks with the same voice of thunder, then why do you take from him the rightful glory of his divine Sonship? For in all his words and actions he is like his Father, and on an equality with him. Every utterance of his has that incontrovertible authority that we find also in his Father, whom all things inevitably obey, things that are not yet in being, as well as things that are. He has equally the right to give commands, the strength to be effective, the swiftness to be effortlessly master.

Does it scandalize you, then, that he was

able to die, that he endured being crucified? But if your eye is not thereby evil because he
Cf. Mt 20:15
is good,* not confused by the immensity of the divine splendor, you will see clearly enough that the cross and death were once Christ's weapons of war, and now they are his banner of triumph. What could display his might more resplendently than to have the power to lay down his life as and when he chose, and to take it up again at the time and
Cf. Jn 10:18
in the manner of his choosing?* What could have been stronger than this death, which was death indeed to all our hateful enemies, death to the devil, death to sin, death to suffering, last of all, death to death?

4. I have good reason, therefore, to compare the power of the Lord Jesus to myrrh. It is a myrrh that both gives life to what is dead and preserves from death what is about to die, both heals what is wounded and keeps safe what is unharmed. Yet much more precious even than this myrrh is the myrrh that bedews the lips of Jesus with healing for the soul rather than the body. This was the myrrh, wonderful in its efficacy, that those men long ago experienced when Jesus said, in a single drop of myrrh, the one sentence, 'Come,
Mt 4:19
follow me.'* In that one moment, they cast aside every last vestige of worldly and corruptible expectations, and they died as far as this world is concerned. Then they set out to follow Jesus, and day by day began to put on more of the youthfulness of a holy incorruptibility.

Then there was the woman who came with an alabaster vase of ointment. Perhaps the lips of Jesus did not speak audibly to her, but deep within her heart they were distilling their dew, and she came to him bathed in it interiorly. She came looking for him who had first come to her, she anointed him who had before anointed her,* and she laid hold of *Cf. Phil 3:12* him who had laid hold of her in the first place.* She had already heard from her tomb *Cf. Jn 11:28* his voice in all its power, summoning her soul to rise again, and a little later her brother, Lazarus, heard the same Lord Jesus, gently calling him too, to rise from his tomb.* *Cf. Jn 11:43*

Finally, to all who are sinners as she was, Jesus opens his mouth to say one word, pregnant with grace, 'Do penance, for the kingdom of heaven is close at hand.'* For this is the *Mt 4:17* beginning of Jesus' preaching, breaking his silence to preach the good news first and particularly to those on whose account he proclaims he was anointed. 'The Spirit of the Lord is upon me,' he said, 'because he has anointed me to preach the good news to the poor,'* 'to bind up the broken hearted.'† If **Lk 4:18 †Is 16:1* he was to heal those who were broken, it was in the highest degree necessary that he himself be copiously anointed by the Spirit of the Lord. He was sent from heaven for this very reason, to take up and anoint the wounds of his poor people.

Consider with what generosity of grace and with what brevity in its dispensation the new lawgiver established his new covenant with sinners. His words were: 'Do penance, for the kingdom of heaven is close at hand.'* *Mt 4:17* From the necks of the weak he lifts off the heavy yoke of the law, he releases the poor from the rich and complex ritual of its sacrifices, he makes their peace with the Lord, but on one sole condition, namely, that they should do penance. He does not merely promise them peace or even pardon, but without further ado sends them straight on to the kingdom, to the kingdom of heaven. But the kingdom of heaven was so far distant, so infinitely above the sick and the weak, that they could not reach it. So he added this grace, too, that, since they had not the strength to come to the kingdom themselves, the kingdom would come to them.

5. This was the first time Jesus opened his mouth, and who would not feel amazement at the unprecedented greatness of the blessing that broke from his lips? Speaking of this kind of word, he himself said very aptly, 'The
Jn 6:64 words that I speak to you are spirit and life.'* A no less fitting description is that of the evangelist: 'All wondered at the words of
Lk 4:22 grace that proceeded from his mouth.'*

But let me come now to the words of wisdom with which, as it is written, he
Cf. Mk 9:30 opened his mouth and taught his disciples.* This too was a choice myrrh, breathing out an indescribably sweet perfume. They were drawn by its perfume and taught by its unction, until it was not wearisome to them to follow Jesus to the mountain country or to sit down there with him. That myrrh also put an abrupt end to any high-flown wisdom or understanding that took any other origin than from the lips of Jesus. In short, those words of wisdom were wonderful not only to the good among his hearers, but to the evil

also, so that all had to say, 'Never has any man spoken like this man.'* And they said, too, 'Where did he get this wisdom?'* And again, 'How does he know letters, never having been taught?'* That wisdom of yours, in fine, is the very Wisdom of God, which is Christ, and that is beyond my reach.*

Jn 7:46
Mt 13:54
Jn 7:15
Cf. Ps 139:6

This wisdom has the marvelous power of making captive and revealing as foolishness any 'wisdom' that sets itself up in opposition to the Wisdom of God. This is equally true whether it is the wisdom of the flesh or of the law or of this world or of the mighty ones of this world.* What does the apostle say? 'Where is the wise man? Where is the scribe? Where is the conqueror of this age?'* And a few words later, he expressly mentions the fourth kind that I spoke of, when he says, 'Among the perfect we speak wisdom, but not a wisdom of this world nor of the mighty ones of this world, who are doomed to pass away.'*

Cf. 2 Cor 10:5
1 Cor 1:20
1 Cor 2:6

6. For there is a 'fleshly wisdom', which, as the apostle also says, 'is hostile to God,' and therefore 'does not obey the law of God, indeed, cannot do so.'* It is wise enough in all that pertains to the flesh, but the joys of spiritual sweetness it neither knows by experience nor seeks through desire. Clearly then, all this is but an animal or brutish wisdom, since it chooses to make its pasture with brute beasts. In fact, it becomes more senseless than the senseless animal, in failing to pursue what is really close to it, and so through its own fault is much less intelligent in every way. In other respects, too, it is

Rom 8:7

much less happy than a beast, because of the penalty it incurs. In short, 'The wisdom of the flesh is death,'* for it buys eternal damnation for the price of a fleeting pleasure.

Rom 8:6

The wisdom of the scribes, too, or of the law, proudly sets itself in opposition to the wisdom of God. It knows nothing of true divine justice, which means to place all reliance on one thing alone, the grace of saving mercy, and it disdains to be subject to the justice of God. It is not possible for it, even, to bow down its neck before the all-powerful God, so thickened is it with the fatty muscle of the stubborn. More and more it stiffens in the rigidity of this stubbornness, as scripture says, 'The pride of those who hate you ascends continually.'*

Cf. Ps 74:23

7. How long, O worldly Israel, will the sinews of your neck be unyielding iron? How long will you be the only one to refuse submission to the gentle yoke of Christ? What is it, I ask you, that makes you bear the shame of so long a slavery? Is it that you do not understand what it means to serve him whose service is the one true freedom?* Why is it that for so long a time now, you have fled from the face of the Lord Jesus to wander aimlessly from one country to another, an exile and a vagabond?* You are growing old in a foreign land, you are polluted by your nearness to the dead, or, which is even more wretched, you are dead yourself, while surrounded by the living. If only, even at this late date, your arrogance would turn upon you with a direct retort, and you would say, 'It is my very wisdom that has led me astray!'* Since I

Cf. Augustine, De quantitate animae *34; PL 32:1078.*

Cf. Gen 4:12

Cf. Is 47:10

'have known how to read letters', therefore I have not 'come in the power of the Lord,'* *Ps 71:16* and therefore I have been driven out of the sanctuary of grace. I have abandoned Jesus, the font of wisdom and the spring of living waters,* *Cf. Jer 17:13* and so my heart has grown dry and I waste away in my thirst even to this day.* *Cf. Ps 102:4*

8. If only the true Wisdom of God, which is Christ, would speak like this to the heart of his handmaid! If only at long last my Lord would speak like this to the heart of Jerusalem,* *Cf. Is 40:2* that she might remember the days of her youth! Then she would return to the bridegroom of her springtime,* *Cf. Joel 1:8* and at last, as in the beginning, the voice of the spouse and the voice of the bride would be heard in the tents of Jacob! May that festal day come at last, a day longed for specially by the entire church, when David will be brought back to Jerusalem with music of cymbal and song! On that happy day the church of all nations, the daughter of Sion, will lead him into the home of his mother, into the chamber of her who bore him.* *Cf. Sg 3:4* She will give a completely new form to the grace he has known in ages past, and for herself, there will be no begrudging her spouse to another's embraces, but a joyful sharing.

On that blessed day Israel will drink from the fountains of Israel, and all the more deeply because of the long delay. Let me say it again, Israel will drink, from its own cisterns, the water which in the past it alone desired to possess, and which now, for so many days, it alone has lost in isolation. But then, after so long, it is to be admitted to that water, and men will drink, and cattle too, and the camels of Abraham will have their fill.* It is right, too, that the one who drank first, when it was the only one who wanted to drink, should now in these present days drink least of all, and in the last days, it will drink last, but then it will not be the only one.

Cf. Gen 24:20

It was very just that the lover of Israel should fall to the lot of the more loving wife, the one who was unwilling to divide the child that was given her but preferred to hand him over intact to the bosom of the very one who had secretly tried to snatch him from her own bosom.* Israel has known a long tribulation, but in the end, however late, it will be anointed from head to foot with the oil of a new grace and will understand what it is hearing. Then instructed as much by the present bride of Jesus as by the spouse himself, it will learn to love Jesus in company with the rest of mankind. Then Israel will call him by the same name that the church does, she who has always been his faithful bride throughout this earthly life, and who cries out to him: 'Your name is as oil poured out.'*

Cf. 1 Kgs 3:26

Sg 1:2

So much for the wisdom of the law.

9. Then we come to the wisdom that those who have conquered this world falsely arrogate to themselves. What can we say of it except that it is as foolish as it is pompous? It vainly prides itself on the name of wisdom, yet has not the least share in wisdom's strength and flavor. The true Wisdom of God took form at a far distance from their eyes, and has the more carefully concealed herself

from them, the more reckless they became in cheapening the glory of that sacred name of hers and in presuming they could break into her treasures through their own power.

10. This swollen self-conceit shows itself in four different shapes. It either probes into the secrets of nature, or into the subtle distinctions of words, or into the foundations of moral behavior, or into the mysteries of divine holiness. Now we are not blaming the pursuit of learning,* as long as it takes its direction from the font of wisdom, flows gently along the riverbed of humility, and then returns again to the font of its origin by practising virtue and by giving thanks.* But when it is a question of 'ascents' of this kind,* great and wonderful beyond the reach of man, and they 'arrange' them in their heart,* and from the power of their own heart, without the help of God, then they have not the guidance of true divine wisdom. Then their course is a headlong one, from this false wisdom into a true folly, from pride into lack of gratitude, from ingratitude into impiety, and from that into that terrible abyss of evils that the apostle inveighed against.*

Cf. Bernard, SC 36.2; SBOp 2:4; CF 7:174.

Cf. 2 Thess 1:3

Cf. Ps 84:7

Cf. Pr 28:26

Cf. Rom 1:29

If we think about it, these may well be the four kinds of 'wise men' that Jeremiah took care to exclude from the sanctuary of the true wisdom. He spoke of 'the Sons of Hagar, who seek after the wisdom that belongs to this earth, the traders from the land of Teman, the story-tellers and the searchers for knowledge and understanding. They have not learnt the way of wisdom, or given thought to her paths.'* He meant those 'who seek after the

Bar 3:23

wisdom that belongs to this earth to stand for the investigators into nature, while he very properly describes as 'story-tellers' the men who devote themselves to the conceits of loquacity! Then he seems to have implied, by 'the searchers after knowledge and understanding', those who argue about moral decency, and who see the invisible things of God made clear to the intellect, through the mir-
Cf. Rom 1:20 ror of the visible creation.*

A little further on he makes mention of that wisdom which Paul called 'the wisdom of
Cf. 1 Cor 2:6 the mighty of this world,'* and says of it, 'There were giants there,' obviously meaning in the great house of God which is the house of wisdom, 'who were famous from the beginning, great in stature, expert in war. God did not choose them, nor give them the way of
Bar 3:26,27 knowledge; and so they perished.'* No one would question that these 'giants, great in stature', are the mighty of this world. They are clearly those giants of the race of Anakim whose attacks the sons of Israel so dreaded when they were about to enter the promised
Cf. Deut 1:28 land.* And because they have been 'expert in war from the beginning', they have overthrown Adam, and in him and with him, his entire race. From then on they set themselves with relentless hatred against all of this race who are anxious to return home to their own land. This is the wisdom of the world's mighty, a wisdom they themselves destroyed for the sake of their splendor, scripture tells
Cf. Ez 28:17 us,* and it is ours too, in as much as we are foolish enough to keep them company by day and by night.

For these are men 'expert in war', and in all the huge exertions war demands. From their youth they have been exercised in continual battle, in immense hardiness, in tireless wickedness. As we leave our mother's womb, poor, peaceloving weaklings, chained, as it were, by mortality and sin, they seize upon us immediately and drag us off to perdition.

This wisdom also, poisonous and death-dealing, the wisdom of God made foolishness, as it does all the others we spoke of before. What is most to be wondered at, it does it in a completely indescribable way, namely in its foolishness totally beyond the mental reach of that earthly wisdom which can only see God's wisdom as stupidity!

11. It was no great thing for God, in his wisdom, to condemn the wisdom of both men and fallen angels. What is exceedingly great and marvelous, though, is this, that, as the apostle says, the foolishness of God should defend for the wisdom of God alone the glory of his Name!* Christ was cruci- *1 Cor 1:25*
fied, and this made him a stumblingblock to the Jews and folly to the Gentiles.* To the *Cf. 1 Cor 1:23*
wisdom of the flesh he was a sign and portent to be met with opposition, while to the cleverness of the fallen angels he was clearly a spectacle of terror and a treacherous snare. So we read in scripture, 'Let treachery come upon them unawares, and let the snare which they hid entrap them, and let them fall to their ruin in its nets'.* No more can any wise *Ps 35:8*
man of whatever kind boast of his wisdom, if he thinks of it by its real name, what Paul called it when he declared that 'the wisdom

of this world is foolishness in the sight of
1 Cor 3:19 God.'* For there is no wisdom, there is no understanding, which does not come from the Lord God, much less one which is contrary to the Lord, which sets itself up in opposition to divine wisdom.

12. Finally, note how the Wisdom of God put to shame, with one word, all the wisdom, or rather lack of it, we have been speaking of. 'If anyone wants to come after me,' he said, 'let him deny himself, take up his cross, and
Mt 16:24 follow me.'* When do you think the palate of carnal wisdom would be able to relish a remark like this? At the very appearance of this saying, would it not immediately teem with inanities, and like the wheel of a cart laden with the hay of fleshly satisfactions, rumble away with the low mutter of, 'This saying is
Jn 6:61 hard, and who can hear it?'* And what of the wisdom of the law, or that of the scribes of bygone times, or that which even today is observed in many of our learned men? These have carried off the key of knowledge, but like the doctors of the law before them, they say and do not do. With proud ambition they pursue a wisdom that is nothing but empty pretentiousness, and they flee far away from
Cf. 1 Cor 1:17 the cross of Christ as from a sign of terror.* Surely, as Christ moves towards his cross and beckons to them, this wisdom seems to answer, 'Depart from me, you are a scandal
Cf. Mt 16:23 to me'?*

Finally, there are those whom Paul calls the mighty of this world, and Jeremiah, the storytellers. At the bitter hearing of this word they are overcome with immediate nausea, as at some abominable food. All the more do they summon back to their own table all who want to hear and follow, crying out, 'Stolen waters are sweeter, and more tasty is bread eaten in secret.'* And again, 'Why listen to him? He is mad.'* Or they say what Ahimelech once said of David, 'Do we lack fools and madmen that you have brought this witless man to me?'*

Pr 9:17
Jn 10:20
Cf. 1 Sam 21:15

Certainly those wise men misinterpret the myrrh of mortification dripping from the lips of Jesus, which we mention in a previous sermon, and, like Ahimelech with the froth on David's mouth, they take it for a sign of madness. This is because 'the unspiritual man does not perceive the things that belong to the Spirit of God, but they are folly to him,' so says the apostle, 'and he is not able to understand them.'*

1 Cor 2:14

The wisdom of the prince of this world, whom scripture describes as more cunning, not only than the sons of light, but also than all beasts, namely, those men we spoke of above,* this very wisdom was wonderfully tricked and deceived when the Wisdom of God distilled from his lips this kind of foolishness! For he said: If this man is the Lord of glory, how is it that he attracts men towards carrying the cross with him, instead of towards the kingdom of glory? But if he himself is come to carry a cross or lay it upon others, how is he the king of glory? In short, if this man is the Son of God, have the angels not received orders about him, to keep the Son of God in all his ways, like the apple of God's eyes, lest he hurt his foot even on a stone?*

Cf. Gen 3:1
Cf. Ps 91:12

Do you think it possible that he whom the Father will not suffer to strike against a stone, should be hurt by the cross or by death? Nevertheless, since because he preaches the cross, he too must be asked about the cross. If he rejects it, he is unwilling to suffer, but if he lets it come to him, he is shown up as inglorious. It will be impossible, indeed unthinkable for him to be deemed the Son of God, when I have put wood in his bread, when the words of his teaching now sweeter than honey to those who hear him, have
Cf. Jer 11:19 become bitter.*

It is quite inevitable that all will repudiate this talk about suffering. It will necessarily
Cf. 1 Cor 1:22 happen that those who seek 'a sign',* will find the cross a scandal, and searchers after wisdom will call it empty folly.

Ps 6:3 13. 'But, O Lord, how long will you be?'* How long will you hold your peace, while the serpent sharpens his tongue like this and hisses in your ears? Let the 'wise' be caught in his own 'wisdom', he prepared a snare, let him be trapped in it, he dug a pit, let him fall into it! You have sent forth from Zion, O Lord,
Cf. Ps 110:2 your rod of power!* Strike the serpent with your rod, though not with its full strength! Clothe your rod in serpent-shape, free of course from venom, but even greater in subtlity! The first serpent, with his devilish cunning, devised the death of the living, he devised what was still more dreadful, the death of Life. The new Serpent has devised the death of the serpent, and from his own death, life for the dying. What more is to be said? In his innocence and simplicity, our most inno-

cent serpent swallowed up all the serpents of Pharaoh,* all the craftiness of the ancient serpent. So the glory of his strength, seemingly lost for the moment, came radiantly back to him, to whom be honor, glory and power for ever and ever. Amen.

Cf. Ex 7:10

SERMON TWENTY-FOUR

The beginning of the twenty-fourth sermon. What grace is conferred when the lips of Jesus are pressed together for a kiss or opened to their full for breathing upon us. Why charity has in it much that is bitter but very salutary, and is for this reason called by the bride the first myrrh.

Sg 5:13 'HIS LIPS DISTILL the first myrrh.'* The previous sermons dealt, as far as God gave the grace, with the first myrrh distilled by the lips of the spouse either in silence or in speech. Now there comes before us the question of what flows from his lips when they are pressed together to give a kiss or opened to their full to breathe forth the Holy Spirit. A sublime theme, far beyond my strength! It calls for loftier powers of intellect and a more eloquent use of language. Still, though a man be richly blessed with both these qualities, if he has not gone to school to the Holy Spirit as a humble disciple of charity, if the living and breathing words of the Spirit have not rung in his ears, then, even should he lift up his voice among us like a *Cf. Is 58:1* trumpet,* as far as we are concerned he would be speaking to the air, tiring himself out to no purpose, and uselessly taking up our time.

So in my own case, who will tell me how

to act, since what I so need is not forthcoming? Lacking experience of holy things puts me in a most difficult position. How am I to give to others when I myself am so painfully inadequate? On what grounds am I made to render an account for something that has not been entrusted to me? Or if I have perhaps laid hold of it in some slight degree, what I hold is so very little that it can scarcely be divided out for sharing.

2. After deep thought, then, you, and I together with you, will question on this matter those who have gone into this doctrine more fully and been more frequently anointed with the most holy kiss of Jesus. He has breathed on them and filled them with his Holy Spirit, so that they have understood how to speak in a way that pleases him. They hand down to us nothing that they have not first read in their own hearts, dictated from the mouth of Jesus, deeply incised with his finger, inscribed by the Spirit of the living God as if in ink. Let us consider, our hearts filled with holy love, those companions of the spouse and bridesmaids of the bride, for example, Gregory, Augustine, Ambrose, and, in our own day, those noble friends of the spouse and attendants to the bride, Bernard, Guerric, Richard, Gilbert, and others like them.* The unction of the Spirit first made these men its pupils, and then made them into teachers. It was in the marriage chamber that they learned to understand the marriage song, and only then did they become able to explain this sacred love to us. Even so, they could hardly expound in words more than the

Those who wrote on the Song of Songs.

slightest part of the great things they had learned in their hearts. Still, I receive them as angels of God, and I listen to them with my whole heart as to Seraphim, a name that is said to mean those who both burn and set others afire.

Their fiery speech is evidence of the fire that is in their hearts.* When they talk of the love of the spouse and bride it is not with stealthy dependence on the experience of others, but with open-handed sharing of their own experience. With men like this the spouse speaks as to intimates. As he says, 'We speak of what we know and we bear witness to what we have seen.'* They are the only ones blessed with a real understanding of what they say, for to have loved means to have understood.

Cf. Bernard, SC *79:1; SBOp 2:272, CF 40:137.*

Jn 3:11

So, as we said, in this matter it is they to whom we must turn for information. It may even be that when the bride speaks of her beloved's lips, it is quite likely she means men like these, since it is he himself who is found to have said to each single one of them, 'If you separate the precious from what is worthless, you will be as my mouth.'*

Jer 15:19

3. In the truest sense, what is worthless is whatever glitters with worldly dignities, whatever delights in riches, whatever finds luxury very appealing, whatever has the brilliance of today's wisdom. It was Truth himself who bore witness to this when he said, 'What is exalted among men is abominable in the sight of God.'* How worthless, if it is not only contemptible in God's opinion, but actually abominable? It not only arouses distaste in him, but even disgust. This therefore is the

Cf. Lk 16:15

work of every such coiner, if he is really to become the mouth of God, to take the greatest care to use the smelting fires of true charity as a means of separating out the precious from the worthless, and of giving everything in his own heart, and then secondarily in the hearts of other men, its proper value.

Listen to what one of God's chosen has to say. Paul declares, 'I count everything as loss . . . . and I count everything as refuse, that I may gain Christ.'* How precious Christ *Phil 3:8* was in Paul's eyes! Compared to Christ, he found everything under heaven too despicable, too noisome, too unworthy even to be mentioned! Here indeed was a worthy mouth, one that spoke of Christ, or, to put it better, one where Christ spoke of himself. If only Christ would raise me to the worthiness of receiving a kiss from this kind of mouth! If only from those lips of his he would distill on me that first purest myrrh, which is the charity of Christ! I would have thought myself happy even to have been blessed with grace from a less pure vessel, until at last the Lord my God should think me ready to become a man he could use as his own mouth to speak of himself.

4. You may perhaps be saying: Why this coupling of charity and myrrh? The one is all overflowing with sweetness, and the other is held to be naturally bitter, which is what gives it its efficacy? Nevertheless, though charity may be exceedingly sweet, yet it knows very bitter loathings of its sweetness. It knows the very sad complaints and heavy delays of

interrupted pleasure. It knows with what great anxiety its desires come to birth, with what difficulty they go forward from their conception, and how wearisome it is to bring them to an issue. Was he not held fast in bitterness who said, 'I was in despair, and my soul chose
Job 7:15 rather to be strangled than to suffer?'* And were not his fingers full of the most excellent myrrh, he who said of himself and his fellows, 'We ourselves who have the firstfruits of the spirit, groan inwardly, indeed, all creation
Rom 23:22 groans and is in labor, even until now'?* And that other voice, too, crying out aloud to the Lord as if suffering violence, 'See how it is for my peace that my bitterness is very
Is 38:17 bitter.'* Then there was the man who contemplated the Lord's glory, and went away bitter, 'in the indignation of his spirit,' and the reason was that the Spirit of the Lord was
Cf. Ez 3:14 with him, giving him strength.* As for Isaiah, he beheld the majesty of God and heard the Seraphim praising the ineffable mystery of the Holy Trinity, one jubilant choir answering another with ceaseless song. But the hearing sent him back to us sad and bitter and full of shame, reviling himself as a man of unclean lips who should not be admitted to hear
Cf. Is 6:5 angelic harmonies.* David likewise, who could call God himself to witness that He loved him, because God heard the cry of his supplicating voice, David too goes on to lament his being surrounded by the snares of death and having
Cf. Ps 116:3 found distress and anguish.*

Then we have the blessed virgin herself, into whom the whole stream of love flowed freely and who holds the teacher's chair par excellence in the school of those who love Jesus. When she bore in her arms the Word of the Father made flesh through her motherhood, and 'her spirit rejoiced in God her Savior,'* that was a rejoicing more than human, more than angelic, too. Yet it was then, all unexpectedly, from the Lord's sanctuary as from an arrow flying in the day,* or rather, as from a sword thrusting deep in the night, that she received, did she not, the wound of a most bitter sorrow? For it was from Simeon's prophecy that she learnt of the passion of her son. This was a blow that could never heal, a bundle of the most bitter myrrh that she carried between her breasts.* It was then that she died with him. We could even say that it was then, before her son was crucified, that she crucified herself because of him.*

Lk 1:47

Cf. Ps 91:5

Cf. Sg 1:13

Cf. Lk 2:35

5. Any soul, therefore, that longs for the joys of love, must not shrink back from its bitterness if it desires to experience its sweetness. The lips of the beloved may be ready to kiss you, and in that kiss you may realize they are distilling myrrh. Do not be so foolish as to reject it, do not offer a reluctant greeting to the grace that comes to you. You have submitted to the yoke of a strangely hothouse sort of love, if you are happy only in its pleasures, and hasten away, all whining and squeamish, from what is involved in the labor of love and must of necessity present themselves to those who walk in love's ways. In short, listen to what is said by the spouse to any soul having the fruit of charity within its womb or even just anxious to have it: 'A

woman has sorrow when she gives birth, for her hour has come. But when she has brought forth her son, she remembers the grief no longer, because of her joy that a son is born
Jn 16:21 into the world.'*

Here we have the law of this child-bearing, one which the lawgiver himself, her spouse, has laid upon her, or rather, made for her. But you know this perfectly well. From your riches 'I did not turn aside, for you made a
Ps 119:102 law for me.'* In other words: I do not turn aside from those aspects of your riches which others complain of as being bitter. By the law of your love, which you have stamped gently and sweetly within my very heart, you have made me ready for everything, and in consequence, all your commands are a delight to me. Anguish may lay hold of us as if we were about to give birth, but then we must be strengthened in the Holy Spirit, knowing that labor pains herald the birth. The more overwhelming the suffering, the closer at hand is the reward, and when it reaches its peak, then suddenly, all grief is blotted out as joy comes flooding in.

6. Yet the pangs of childbirth are not without their own benefits, even with all their pain. First of all, the loving heart sees its desolation as a rebuke, and is forced by necessity to think the reason for it is its own unworthiness and lack of likeness to God. It feels compelled to say to itself, 'Why, I wonder, has my Lord not visited me with his accustomed grace? He came neither yesterday nor the day before. Where is the usual comfort of a deep, satisfying prayer, where the rich

holocausts of an outpouring of love, where the overwhelming happiness of secret rejoicing, where, most of all, where is Jesus, in whose presence I once always lived, and now remember it with such sorrow? Oh, what has happened? Why has famine taken the place of my happy plenty, mourning of joy, dryness of devotion and a thick cloud hiding the life-giving light? My unhappiness is crushing, as the prophet says, 'the shadows of evening lengthen,'* and a lengthening, habitual night has cut off the light of divine consolation. I run after Jesus, calling and crying, I go after him loudly pleading with him to come back to me, and as if I were like Pilate and he had some reason not to speak to me, he answers me not a word.* Surely he would not turn from me without reason, and surely the reason must be my own fault?

Jer 6:4

Cf. Mk 15:5

I have experienced how good he is, how frequently he has dealt kindly with his servant.* He is still the same, though now he seems harsh to me, and I still believe, and hold with absolute certainty, that in to the radiant brightness of his everlasting goodness, no stain could ever come. Rather let me rage, and rightly so, against my own dullness of heart, my own sluggishness, my own bitterness. I have tasted wisdom so often, yet I find myself still so insipid. The Sun of justice has shone on me so often, yet I feel myself as hard as baked clay. I seem to have come away from the sweetness of the heavenly manna with nothing but a mouth more bitter than before.

Cf. Ps 119:65

On that day of glorious happiness, when I

sat down with the Lord Jesus at his supper
and held in my hand some part of his own
Cf. Lk 24:42 honeycomb,* do you think some sort of
dying fly could have fallen onto the mouthful
I was about to swallow? I mean something
like ingratitude, pride, anger or envy? How
I fear that perhaps that loving eye saw me
attacking the feast with far too little
self restraint, that my great delight in
him was lacking in reverence, that I laid hands
upon more than was fitting. 'You have found
honey,' says Solomon, 'eat what is fitting for
you, or you may overeat and lose the honey
Pr 25:16 through being sick.'*

If I should want to justify myself, the
poverty I feel at present, and the hunger in
which I have languished so many days already,
reprove me for my arrogance. Granted that
Cf. 1 Cor 4:4 I am not aware of anything against myself,*
but God has certainly found out the guilt
Cf. Gen 44:16 of his servant.* So he hides his face from
Cf. Is 8:17 me,* and treats me as my foolishness de-
Cf. Pr 26:4 serves.*

What can I do, then? I shall wait patiently
Cf. Ps 40:1 for the Lord, until he notices me.* If he
seems slow, I shall nonetheless take my stand
Cf. Hab 2:3,1 with the prophet to keep watch.* I shall place
perfect confidence in the goodness that is his
by nature, because he will always be alert to
the cry of the poor man who abandons him-
Cf. Ps 22:24 self to him.* He will find time for me, too,
but only when he sees it is right, and that
I need it. Meanwhile, as far as is in me, I will
endure my Lord's delay as if it were myrrh, a
very bitter but very efficacious medicine for
my wounds. I will rub my flesh all over with

it, and I will put to death my members which are on this earth.* And what kind of fragrance is more exquisitely adapted to this end than myrrh? *Cf. Col 3:5*

7. Indeed, 'love is not jealous or spiteful, it is not arrogant or ambitious, it does not insist on its own way, it is not irritable or resentful, it does not rejoice in the wrong, but rejoices in the right.'* Here we have a beautiful example of how the myrrh of charity puts to death the members of that body which the apostle calls 'the body of sin,'* and how it kills in the body the worms of corruption. Envy makes the virtues rot, Solomon tells us,* and it is envy, according to Paul, which breathes its last when it meets the scent of charity, which 'is not jealous'. The natural daughter of an envious disposition is spite, which tarnishes all that is bright and good, and like the moth, eats away even what is strongest. But it cannot bear the fragrance of goodness, and so it is snuffed out immediately when anointed with charity, which 'is not spiteful', and covers over the spiteful deeds of others. *1 Cor 13:4-7* *Cf. Rom 6:6* *Cf. Pr 14:30*

Pride is the work of the moths that destroy grace, eating away, not what is my neighbor's, just what is my own. In one moment it swallows what took much hard work to achieve. But this too, vanishes at the scented breath of charity, which has no desire to be 'arrogant' but only to be a humble emptiness that God will fill. Ambition is the ignoble fruit of pride, shunning true glory and craving for vain-glory, yet this also disappears at the sight of this myrrh, for 'charity is not ambitious'!

Then there is greed, intent on its own profit and uninterested in profiting anybody else. As soon as charity breathes on it, it dies like a worm vulnerable to a wholesome unction, for 'charity does not insist on its own way, but seeks that of others'. And anger is a worm, too, first eating out its own heart, and then devouring the hearts around it, a worm that charity, which 'is not irritable', blows out of existence with the lightest of puffs. Last of all, is that unhealthy worm, suspicion, a shrill nurse, quick to probe out evil and persuasive in entering into it. Once it has begun to gnaw, it does not easily subside, but when charity, which 'is not resentful', awakes, it immediately closes its eyes in sleep.

8. There are other gifts of grace, and each one of them has its own special power to exterminate this kind of worm, but quite definitely, charity is the first of the gifts. Its sway is far greater, its quality is finer, and it is more solid in its effect. So the bride has every reason for calling it 'the purest myrrh'. For whatever the other virtues do individually, each one healing some one disease, charity heals the whole lot all in one, and does it with greater force and graciousness. This is the king among the unctions, not only for its pleasing power, but for its invaluable grace.

In a word, it is the spouse who makes use of charity, and like a true spouse, he presses it upon his bride to effect her cure. He intends to heal her by nothing else than the favor of his kiss and the sweet breathing of his Spirit.

Therefore the bride herself has no other desire than to have all her sickness cured by this one remedy, that he should kiss her with the kiss of his mouth,* or else enrich her ever more fully with his princely Spirit. Not that a kiss of such majesty could possibly be either given or understood without an inpouring of the Holy Spirit, but the breath of Jesus is drawn from the very depth of his heart, and so comes with an indefinable strength and vehemence. Those men on whom he once breathed the Holy Spirit, received charity and also power to forgive the sins of other men as well. According to the measure meted out to them by God, the salvation they had freely received, they were freely to administer to all.*

Cf. Sg 1:1

Cf. Mt 10:8

In the kiss, then, a richer sweetness is instilled, in the breathing of the Spirit, a greater strength. Love is sweetened by one, strengthened by the other. One deepens desire, the other fashions steadfastness, encourages generosity. In pleading for both, the bride always has at hand the twofold petition of her spouse to his Father: 'Give me the joy of your salvation, and uphold me with a princely spirit.'* Let us, too, however unworthy, make this same twofold prayer, and may we be graciously heard by the Father of our Lord Jesus Christ, who with this same only begotten Son and the Holy Spirit, lives and reigns, God, for ever and ever. Amen.

Ps 51:12

SERMON TWENTY-FIVE

The beginning of the twenty-fifth sermon. How there are two ways in which the hands of the spouse may be 'rounding', that is, either made round in a lathe, or making round in a lathe. How well suited to the Word who became man and suffered for our sakes, are the wheel, the art, and the whole business of rounding off in a lathe. What are the five fingers of the Spouse's left hand.

'HIS HANDS ARE TURNED GOLD, filled with hyacinths.'* In celebrating the beauty of the most beautiful of the sons of men,* the bride pays great attention to the order of her praises, arranging each phrase with skill. After the lips, she turns naturally to the hands, a wise decision, since it is on those lips alone that grace is poured out and, equally, in those hands alone that the fullness of virtue resides. So I repeat, after the lips, the hands form a very fitting topic for praise, since on this very point we have the words of scripture, 'He spoke, and these things were done.'* Whatever proceeds from those lips, whether the wisdom of conversation, the modesty of silence, the love shown by a kiss or the steady strength of breathing, whatever the virtue may be that

Sg 5:14

Cf. Ps 45:2

Ps 33:9

goes forth from those lips, it cannot be ineffective. He speaks, and then he acts. First he gives the inspiration for what has to be done, but also, of necessity, he does what has been inspired.

First of all, however, let us cast a superficial glance, if that is agreeable, over the general structure of these words of eulogy. Then let us draw back the sacred veil, so that the very shape of the truth may issue forth with greater splendor.

2. Three statements are made in praise of these hands: that they are 'rounded', that they are 'golden', that they are 'filled with hyacinths'. The bride says they are 'golden', because she wants to commend either their warm glowing color or their immense power and vast wealth. Next she quotes them as 'filled with hyacinths', to heap up proof of their generosity. These are hands pouring out from their fullness with utmost liberality, and yet nothing of that fullness is ever diminished. Their inexhaustible resources are constantly drawn upon without falling below strength in the slightest.

But now she speaks of 'rounded', and here she is addressing herself and her spouse. For in this instance, she makes no sense as far as we are concerned. When she says 'rounded', does she mean 'rounded in a lathe'? Or rather, are they the hands of a turner, because they are quick at this art and apply themselves to the craft of making things round and smooth? For we use the word to describe not only something rounded by the lathe but also to describe the craft by which such work is produced. Which of these meanings is more correct is not clear, but the Wisdom of God is accustomed for this very reason to speak to us in parables and riddles so that the fertile obscurity of his meaning may light up for us a lamp of many facets. For here one meaning does not exclude the other, but both dovetail into each other, joined together like wings that will raise us up to things above us.

3. All that has been said refers to the literal meaning of the words. Now let us knock at the bed-chamber of the spouse and his bride, seeking to have it opened to us.

First we must learn what the bride wished to convey to us by the 'hands' of her spouse. She partly hints at it in another place where her meaning is clearer, though still figurative, and she says, 'His left hand is under my head,
Sg 2:6 and his right hand will embrace me.'* For the hand of the spouse is that twofold work of his, whereby he accomplishes the salvation of his bride upon the earth, and never ceases to work for all eternity. For his Father 'labors
Jn 5:17 until now, and I too,' he says, 'labor.'* So the spouse works for the complete salvation of the bride, one hand making her holy, and one hand bringing her to glory. The former is the left hand, the latter is the right.

4. 'Long life is in the right hand, but in
Pr 3:16 the left hand are riches and honor.'* The bride waits with great joy for the embrace of his right hand, when the glory of her spouse will be revealed. Then 'her husband will be known in the gates, when he sits with the
Pr 31:23 elders of the land,'* sitting on his throne of

majesty, and 'long life' will form a great ring all around her, glowing with the glory of eternity. But here in this present life, it is on the left hand of her beloved that she gently lays her head.

Happiest of women, to be given such a pillow! On her couch, resting upon that pillow, what visions must fill her head, how wakeful her slumber, how sweet her sleep! When she drowses, her spouse keeps ever watchful guard above her, protecting her slumbers from any disturbance or disquiet. Surely the left hand of the spouse abounds in 'riches and glory', when he opens wide to his bride the riches of salvation, the treasuries of holiness, and makes her rejoice in them, like one who has found all riches? And what a weight of glory is laid upon her, too, coming from the testimony of a good conscience and the hope of sharing the glory of the sons of God,* quite apart from the supreme privilege of being wedded to a spouse so gloriously great! *Cf. Rom 5:2*

So the left hand is glorious indeed, yet not as magnificently so as is the right. In the right hand is the fullness of justice, as scripture tells us: 'Your right hand is full of justice.'* However in the time and place assigned to earning our reward, it is the left hand that is specially active, while the right hand has for its sphere the task of apportioning glory, of gathering together the sons of God and distributing to them their inheritance. *Ps 48:11*

Furthermore, those hands were shaped for the only Son of God as if they had been rounded off by a certain skilful use of the

turner's lathe. From the workshop where this craft is practised, they were to go out as craftsmen themselves, fashioning our salvation. For, as the apostle says, because 'he himself has suffered and been tempted, he is able
Heb 2:18 to help those who are tempted.'* It is the Father of the spouse who rounded these hands, and yet the spouse himself, like the son of a workman, worked vigorously with his Father at this most excellent of crafts. Marvelous craftsman, who fashioned his own self so as to refashion us!

5. 'I shall thank you for ever,' Lord
Ps 52:9 Jesus, 'for what you have made.'* You have made yourself into my salvation, you have made me into a prized possession through your salvation. You have made yourself hands in order to save me, made them with skilful artistry, with speed, too, yet with toilsome labor. First of all, like a wise designer, you raised a workshop for this craft of yours, the soul of your virgin mother, and her holy womb. A sublime workshop, vast enough for so great a craft and able to contain so immense a craftsman! But it would be truer to say that she herself, like the valiant woman,
Cf. Pr 31:19 put out her hand to mighty things,* wisely working along with the Wisdom of God in the work of our salvation.

6. Since, then, the bride decided, by the Spirit of God, to adopt the image of this craft when praising her spouse, there will be more of devotion than idle curiosity in lingering a little over it.

The craftsman sits with a piece of wood suspended above him, and another, connected to the first by a thong, under one foot; by a movement of his other foot he raises and lowers the beam. Equally, the wood which is to be rounded is girded by the same thong, connected from the crossbeam in the centre, and so is in precisely the right position to be kept continually turning round in a circle as the foot moves up and down. Moreover, the craftsman has a chisel in his hand, and with firmness and great accuracy he brings this to bear on what is to be shaped, all his movements controlled by a craftsmanship that has become instinctive to him. So the work proceeds with great swiftness, and revolution follows on revolution so quickly that it outstrips the keenness of the eye and baffles the mind.

If we look for the underlying significance of this image, we find two beams of wood, very far removed from each other. One is exceedingly high, towering over our heads, and the other lies prostrate down below. In other words, here are the two natures, the Word and the flesh, which the unimaginable love of God bound marvelously into a unity. So God's love is the thong, imperishable, and it binds with a knot that can never be untied, using for the purpose a certain natural quality, namely, the rational soul. Thus it connects the higher nature and the lower by an ingenious alliance.

Moreover, from the time of this most holy union, each nature is so utterly faithful to this great alliance, that in the lowliness of the flesh, the Word stoops humbly down, and in the sublimity of his majesty, lowliness is lifted

up on high. In a spirit of humility, a man may enter the holy temple of God with the desire to glorify the Lord our God. But God is not pleased with him and does not look with favor on his offering, unless he worships his foot-
Cf. Ps 99:5 stool, for that, too, is holy.* 'Honor loves the
Ps 99:4 king's judgment,'* and this is the law, that the humanity, united to the majesty of the Word, is so taken up into the oneness of the Person, that it can even share impartially in his glory. Yet however much one position succeeds another, whether it raises itself on high or the divine Wisdom comes down low, this same humanity is truly in charge as the craftsman of the whole, pursuing our salvation. The business of our salvation is all arranged by the hand of Wisdom.

Behind every detail in this undertaking stands this aim, it is supremely the object of God's interest and intention. It was conceived in his mind from all eternity and for a long while he revolved it in his thoughts. Then, at the appointed time of salvation, he turned it in bringing it to fulfillment.

And it was his will to work with the chisel of self-control. Indeed, the manner in which a lathe is operated seems of necessity to demand that the salvation which sensuality had violated should be restored by suffering. So the craftsman devotes himself to his work, pressing on with it from morning until
Cf. Gen 3:19 night, in the sweat of his brow.* He labors
2 Cor 11:27 'in toil and hardship, in hunger and thirst,'* in weariness and fear and sadness. How many hated and slandered the work he had begun, trying to pry his hands away from it! But the

workman has an omnipotent title, and whoever strives to resist him, is laid low on his knees. He hastens then, unimpeded in his speed, to the allotted task of our salvation. It lies in the hands of a very great artist, yet he cannot bring it to perfection by a shortcut. It must spread itself out through great and countless turnings of the lathe, and the time it will take will be many days. The Word made flesh did not hasten all the way down to us only to hasten back again at once to where he had been before. No, he came to make his dwelling among us. He who had been with the Father from the beginning, from now onwards became God with us, Emmanuel.* *Cf. Jn 1:14*

7. And so, in the mystery of the Incarnation of the Word, from the very first moment there was nothing useless, nothing transitory, nothing unbeneficial, nothing, in short, that was not full of salvation. The Word himself is full of grace and truth,* and so is everything connected with him. Therefore, whatever is connected with the eternal Word of God, in a marvelous way makes its way back to what we might call the circle of eternity. Whatever was done in passing, by him and in him, those things become truly eternal, as befits the nature of the doer and the purpose of his deeds. In a word, while a circle is in the process of being formed, it cannot be without beginning or end, but once it is complete, it is revealed as having neither beginning nor end. *Cf. Jn 1:14*

At his very first coming to us, our Saviour overflowed with the riches of salvation. Not only did he disentangle human nature from

the law of sin to reconcile it to its creator, but he went so far as to unite it to its creator. What must have been added, then, what greatness of saving power, by the grace of having him actually live among us for so long a time? What of that long imprisonment in his mother's womb, when he submitted to the normal process of gestation and waited patiently for his mother's pregnancy to reach its full term? What of that lowly birth in a wayside lodging, in rags, laid in a manger? What of the crying and weeping of that tender age, which even then he was offering to the Father of mercies for our sins, with a
Cf. Heb 5:7 loud cry,* enormously advancing the work of our salvation? What of the sharp pain of circumcision? What of the protection needed so that he might escape by night? What of his long years of foreign exile in Egypt? What of those thirty years of silence, and then, after his silence, the fruitfulness with which he preached the gospel message? What of the humility of his sacred passion, to pass over everything else, what of his gentleness, his long-suffering, his charity? In all of these, and from each single one of these, has there not flowed forth for us a great stream of holiness and salvation? And all this time it was his left hand that was at work, or rather, that was rounded for us by the long workmanship of the lathe, perfected by ever greater and more skilful efforts.

8. Moreover, although this hand once spread out the heavens, and all the ends of the earth lie enclosed within its grasp, yet it has now become narrowed and shortened by the turner's art, in order to suffer for me.

'Is the hand of the Lord shortened,' said the prophet, 'so that he is unable to save?'* *Is 59:1* Very far from it, but precisely for this very purpose, to become all the more apt and strong to save! For this very purpose superb craftsmanship made it more powerful because of its weakness and more living because of its death. Long before, David, father of the Lord Jesus, according to the flesh, had perceived this, and impatience of the prolonged time of waiting made him exclaim to his Son, 'Let your hand be ready to help me.'* *Ps 119:173* And we find David saying to the Father of the Word, 'Let your hand be on the man of your right hand, and on the son of man whom you yourself made strong.'* *Ps 80:17* So the left hand of the spouse, whether turning or turned, was weakness, taken up on our behalf and from our midst.

Although 'there is no end to his greatness',* *Ps 145:3* that hand was skillfully contracted, as was said above, into a small fistful, yet still filled with salvation. There was no power that this weakness did not have, for 'the weakness of God is stronger than men.'* *1 Cor 1:23* Would you care to hear how strong it is? 'When I am lifted up from the earth,' he says, 'I shall draw all things to myself.'* *Jn 12:32* A strong weakness indeed, when everything in heaven and earth is drawn and contracted to one place, enclosed in the fist of one hand! Through this weakness, the Lord God of vengeance is drawn to mercy, while man, drawn up out of hell, is reconciled to the Father by the cross and drawn even to his fatherly embrace. It is this weakness which crucified our old man with

itself, which formed us into a new man, which triumphed mightily over the powers of the air. It rejoiced the heavens as much by the splendor with which it overthrew the enemy as by its rescue of man. Blessed be the Lord my God, who would reconcile the world to himself in Christ, and thus trained his hands
Cf. Ps 144:1 to battle and his fingers to war!*

9. 'Who has hung the weight of the earth',
Is 40:12 says Isaiah, 'from his three fingers?'* Who if not he who surrendered his soul to death and
Cf. Is 53:12 chose to be counted with the wicked?*
Cf. Job 7:15 Indeed, 'his soul chose to be hung on high',* and the one whom the Lord blessed hung the enormous weight of the whole earth from his threefold suffering. That is, he was condemned, he was crucified, he died. It was not within the power of accusing Juda or the rioting crowd or Pilate the judge to lift that weight greater than heaven and earth. It was he himself, the Lord of hosts, who with three fingers, as said above, lifted it with the greatest ease and lightness. This he did by presenting himself freely to those judges to be condemned, of his own accord surrendering to the gibbet to be crucified, willingly at the last, bowing his head in death.

Somebody may make a difficulty here about there being only three fingers; the left hand of the spouse has two fingers more, from his very earliest days among us, namely, his neediness and his poverty. This is why he cries to his Father, 'I am poor and in need,
Ps 70:5 help me, my God.'* There was no doubt about his need. Although he was free in every respect, he deliberately placed his neck under

the heavy yoke of Adam. So that he might bring relief to hunger and thirst, to cold and heat and weariness and all similar privations, he wanted to be in need of common comforts. And he was truly poor. Although the earth belonged to him and all its fullness,* yet, coming into his own, he wanted to have nothing for his own, not even the smallest of resting places on which to lay his head.* By his neediness he both deceived the prince of this world and showed himself our brother, not just by his compassion, but by actually suffering along with us as a brother should. By his poverty, too, he trampled underfoot the principalities of this world, together with their prince. He summoned his brothers to a more sublime kingdom and clothed himself with poverty, more precious than all riches.

Cf. Ps 24:1

Cf. Lk 9:58

Consequently, by submitting to an unjust sentence, he was victorious, as scripture says, when he was judged.* He was victorious over the injustice of this world's prince, and by the very fact that the just one accepted an unjust condemnation, 'he brought forth our vindication like the light, and our righteousness like the sun at noon.'* Then, by being crucified, he crucified the world's sin, together with its maker. He fastened the sign of the cross to our foreheads and also traced it upon our breasts, so that we may glory 'in nothing except in the cross of our Lord Jesus Christ.'* Lastly, by dying, he made full satisfaction to the eternal Creditor for the common debt of the human race, and wonderfully inspired his brothers, now free, to drain the selfsame chalice.*

Cf. Ps 51:4

Cf. Ps 37:6

Gal 6:14

Mk 10:38

Here, then, we see five types of weakness, and conspicuous in them, five types of strength. It is overwhelmingly a strength 'trained for battle', especially since, as the prophet points out, 'There', that is, in weak-
Hab 3:4 ness, 'strength lies hidden.'* How fitting and wise it was, therefore, that the bride, before going to sleep, should place that hand
Cf. Sg 2:6 beneath her head,* so that all night, while she slept, there might be so many mighty proofs of his special love in her heart, keeping watch there. This is why the bride herself speaks of keeping watch, when she says, 'I go
Sg 5:2 to sleep, but my heart is watchful.'* This is well said, for if the left hand of the spouse is under her head now, in this present life, then she can be absolutely certain that his right hand will embrace her in the life to come. Together with her, may we be found worthy to be given a share in that glory, through the spouse of the church, our Lord Jesus Christ, who, with the Father and the Holy Spirit, lives and reigns, God, for ever and ever.

Amen.

§

A NOTE ON PARAGRAPH THREE

'It was through his great condescension that he united that man to himself'.

In several places in this sermon John of Ford asserts that the Word and the man Jesus were united. He insists that, 'the man was taken up into the glorious union with the Word of God'. *Primus est uidelicet quod in gloriosam Verbi unionem homo ille assumptus est, et hic pollex dexterae huius dici potest, quod in ea digitis omnibus uirtute ac dignitate preapolleat.* Obviously he cannot mean that Christ existed as a man in this world before he was united to the Word. Such a teaching would be contrary to the whole tradition of christological doctrine and would of course be heretical. Because of this John of Ford could certainly not have taught it. Later in the sermon he gives an indication of the correct interpretation of his words: *'Eadem prorsus hora eodemque momento et maiestas est inclinata et prouecta humanitas; et dum Unigenitus Dei factus est filius hominis, filius itidem hominis factus est profecto Vnigenitus Dei.'* In other words, at the moment of his conception the Word took a human nature in the womb of the Virgin Mary. God became man. It was this human nature that was united to the Word at the very moment of its coming into existence. But it was not a human nature that lacked something. John is insisting that Jesus Christ was fully a man with all the faculties and powers of other men. But he is also insisting that it was this precise human nature, *this* man, that the Word raised to union with himself. He is therefore emphasizing strongly that there is something utterly unique about this human nature of Christ. He had a unique intellect, unique powers of observation, unique strength of will, etc. What at first sight might startle the reader becomes on reflection a fine and delicate theological insight.

SERMON TWENTY-SIX

The beginning of the twenty-sixth sermon. Of the left hand of the spouse, which means his passion, and the four dimensions of his cross, where, in passing, there are a few words about the love of spiritual fathers and of sons for their fathers.

Sg 5:14

'HIS HAND IS ROUNDING GOLD, filled with hyacinths.'* I must admit, Lord Jesus, that I stand perplexed, not knowing which of your two hands I should turn to first or more eagerly, to render thanks. And if you should perhaps solve this problem for me, I find the very response itself is beyond me. As far as I am concerned, this is not to be wondered at. I am completely lacking in the riches of charity, and I make my threadbare way to the gates of rich men's houses, begging from door to door my daily bread. Yet these very men of wealth, they too discover that they cannot worthily give thanks for either of the Lord's hands. They can only confess their poverty, because they cannot render him one thing for the thousands he has rendered them.*

Cf. Job 9:3

But if some soul, whatever it may be, from awareness of this divine charity, be confident of making some return however small, it is truly blessed; for the father of the spouse must have betrothed it to his only-begotten in the richest of love, and the spouse himself endowed it with the fulness of his Spirit. True enough, but if I am to speak from my own poverty of myself and others like me, what are we to do?

2. If we look at this most loving of spouses, we see both his hands working equally together, and likewise, each almost contending to forestall the other in labor and care in the exertion, and workmanship our salvation demanded. They make themselves so accessible, they so stretch themselves out and hold themselves extended, that we have good reason to fear that we are about to be utterly overwhelmed by a kindness so manifold and so mighty. To the one hand we are indebted in that we are redeemed by Christ, and to the other in that we are glorified in Christ. The work of the one hand is the love of the dying Christ, yet the other is the splendor of him rising and raising us up together with himself. This one meant death for our death, that one new life for our life. There my Lord became much lower than the angels, much lower than men, too, lower than sinners.* But here, clothing himself with glory and honor, he was raised up on high with the greatest majesty.* Therefore, 'your right hand, O Lord, was raised up in strength,'* evidently because your left hand was narrowed by weakness during your passion. Through your right hand, 'in the greatness of your glory you laid low the enemy,'* an enemy that had first been humbled in the greatness of your humility.

Cf. Ps 8:5
Cf. Ps 104:2
Ex 15:6
Ex 15:7

So both your hands, united in strength and the most delicate artistry, in different ways but with equal passion and the same great love, totally consecrated and poured themselves out in the work of my salvation.

3. Quite correctly, the bride speaks of these hands as 'gold' not as 'gilt'. Without doubt, they are heavy with love, not so much possessing a great deal of love, but possessing all the love there is. They are gold because they have the full substance of love, its matter and its form. They are gold because everyone to whom they reveal themselves, they irradiate with the marvelous, glowing splendor of divine love.

Yet they are also 'filled with hyacinths', for they are brimming over with heavenly blessings. However wide open they seem for giving, or rather, lavishly outpouring, nonetheless, they are still 'filled with hyacinths'. So the love of those hands knows no measure, their richness and abundance escapes far beyond all limitation. And the hyacinth is fittingly placed before us, it has the color of heaven, and heavenly things know nothing of the impoverishment of mutability or the ravages of time. So, too, precious stones, like the hyacinth gem, lose nothing of their value through old age; perhaps they even become more lovely and more worthy of admiration. So the hands of the spouse are filled with hyacinths and thus they may fill the treasury of the bride with heavenly and eternal works, never to be fatigued or diminished even for the slightest moment by this work of outpouring.

And now, where am I to find praise and thanksgiving for all these things, O Lord, my God? Where am I to find that eager perseverence in praying and interceding so that I may take to myself, from his saving hands a gift of salvation from either, from the one that I be justified and from the other that I receive the happiness of heaven.

4. First of all, then, I turn to you, O left hand of my Master. You earned for me the firstfruits of salvation by your labors. To you I owe the firstfruits of this small harvest of charity within me. And even if I pour out on you the whole of this love unreservedly, I should still have done nothing great, nothing worthy of you. You are the rich and towering shrine of my riches for, as Solomon says, in you are all riches and honor.* In very truth, *Cf. Pr 8:18* in you is the whole price of my redemption. All the stripes and all the grief, all the insult and contumely, all the hatred and persecution, all the cursing and mockery, all the poverty and helplessness, all the depths of my Lord's weakness, here they are all stored up as in one vast heap. These are precious treasures, beyond appraisal, yet only stored until one comes who can appraise them, one who is a wise merchant.

These treasures are so hidden, so inscrutable that no human power, no wisdom of flesh and blood, is able to penetrate into their depths. Even if a man should be found to break through to them, he would be blessed if he were not shocked and dismayed at their sight.* For when first seen, they do not *Cf. Mt 11:6* appear desirable, but rather contemptible.

Only in heaven is there one who can rightly
appraise them, the Father of the Only-
begotten Son, and he to whom the Father
Cf. Mt 11:27 choses to reveal them.* But he has revealed
them to the bride of this same Son, and this is
why she says, 'His left hand is under my
Sg 2:6 head.'* And in another place, 'My beloved is
to me a bundle of myrrh, lying between my
Sg 1:12 breasts.'* There were others, too, as scripture
tells us, to whom he made the same revela-
tion: 'There stood by the cross of Jesus his
mother, Mary, and his mother's sister, Mary
Jn 19:25 Cleophas, and Mary Magdalen.'* The disciple
whom Jesus loved stood there also, close
beside the Lord's mother.

5. To 'stand by the cross of Jesus' seems to me an act of the very highest worth. To 'stand by the cross of Jesus' means to be with the blessed mother of Jesus and the bride of the Word, and with the companions of his bride, and to lift one's eyes to the crucified, fixing them there, while pondering on these treasures of immense love with a very deep sense of devotion. If only there was some way by which we too could become worthy to be counted among this company, sharers in their blessedness! Yet the name of 'mother' or 'bride' may be applied quite justly to anyone who is moved by motherly affection to bring forth and train sons for God, anyone who has entered completely into the pure love of the Word, and so cries with continual longing to
the Father, 'Let him kiss me with the kiss
Sg 1:1 of his mouth!'* If anyone is blessed with
both these gifts, so that zeal for his brothers'
salvation is no hindrance at all to the exercise

of divine love, and love for God is no obstacle to the duty of saving others, then that man is not simply blessed, he is obviously very specially and greatly blesssed.

A man like this has won for himself a place next to the cross of Jesus, a very close place, one next to the Lord's mother, who was both mother and bride to the only Son of God. He, too, will take his stand by the crucified one 'in a garment of cloth of gold',* to see if, like *Cf. Ps 45:9* the queen of lovers, he can lay hold of the Lord who has laid hold of him.* *Cf. Ph 3:12*

Next to him comes John, that intimate of the Lord's heart, to represent the virginal life of the saints who keep themselves wholly for Christ. Mary of Cleophas, bound in holy wedlock, expresses the great throng of faithful married people, while Mary Magdalen represents the blessed host who have made reparation by their repentance. All these people, therefore, coming to the cross of Christ with like purpose and approaching the throne of grace with confidence, are allotted *Cf. Heb 4:16* places suitable to the degree of their merits beside the cross. They stand, and they yearn with all their heart, so that in some way they may understand the length and breadth and height and depth of the wonderful charity of Christ.* And to have yearned for this is in *Cf. Eph 3:18* a sense to have mastered it. Indeed, every single one of them makes haste to master all these things, each according to his own capacity.

6. Yet that overflowing charity exceeds, in each one of its dimensions, all the power of human capacity. There is no end to its

length, for it is eternal, nor to its breadth, for it has extended as far as death, even to death on the cross. There is no end to its height, for it has been raised up to the heavens, and beyond them, too. And as far as it is raised, so also it raises us, wonderfully joining us, not only to the angels, but even to God himself. There is no end to its depth, for the lowliness and compassion with which Christ washed us from the stains of our sins in his own precious blood, is completely beyond the understanding of men, and of angels, likewise.

Each of those who stand by the cross lays hold of each and all of these dimensions. Yet I think the measurement of length belongs in a special manner to the mother of Jesus and those whom it is her function to represent, though perhaps 'measurement' is hardly the word when there is nothing but immensity! By that time the sword had already pierced
Cf. Lk 2:35 right through her soul,* but to prevent it from striking too violently and freely, she had for a while to control the fierce attack of its fury by gazing steadily at the everlasting love of God. She had to lay on that bitterest of wounds that sovereign remedy that comes from God's eternal good-pleasure.

John, however, and the disciples whom Jesus loves in him and with him, open their hearts more widely to understand the breadth, reflecting, according to that saying of Jesus mentioned by John, that his greatest love consisted in this that he laid down his life
Cf. Jn 15:13 for his friends.* Paul seems to have understood this even more widely, since he says that it was at a time when we were enemies,

that Christ died for us in all our lovelessness.* *Cf. Rom 5:8* But this refers wholly to this same breadth of love. The Lord Jesus was love, nothing but love, he loved his own who were in the world, and he loved them to the death.* *Cf. Jn 13:1* That they were enemies was completely forgotten, he did not even want to touch upon it. So he would not allow them to be called 'servants' any longer.* *Cf. Jn 14:15* In his eyes, as scripture says, they had become precious and honored,* *Cf. Is 43:4* and from now on they were to bear in his presence an honored name.

Mary of Cleophas, on the other hand, and that great crowd of the faithful whom she represents, stretch themselves most towards understanding that love in its height. By the gift of faith and the grace of God they lift themselves up to a height they know they could never reach through their own power. So they humbly lift up their heads to the height of Christ's love, and so make a ladder for themselves out of Christ's cross.

Then there is Mary Magdalen and her blessed company of penitents. Some of them hold Jesus' head and throw their arms round his body, but she as ever holds and anoints Jesus' feet, that is, she ponders with deep attention the humility and gentleness of such great love.

7. I feel that here I cannot pass over that sweetest of reminders given to the Lord's mother and to John about the unity of reciprocal love. For Jesus specially bent his eyes on them from the cross and said, 'Woman, behold your son,' and then to John, 'Behold your mother.'* *Jn 19:26-7* For me, dearest brothers,

these words of the crucified have a particular meaning, indicating, that with his cross and death as witness, he has set his seal to a perpetual treaty of love between you and myself. For what could more powerfully urge me to love you than this reminder that your father has given you to me as a last bequest, not just as my brothers, but as my sons, since you are
Cf. Eph 5:1 the beloved sons of God?* What joy is there for me now except in you? You have fallen to my lot as a gift from a mighty Father, so that you may be my pledge before God, my
Ph 4:1 flesh-and-blood, 'my joy and my crown'.* And he was far from rejecting you–though he gave you to me–especially when those words sounded from the cross, when your loving mother brought you painfully to birth. Therefore, in giving me so much, he took not the smallest thing from you.

If this interests you, I feel not so much that the honor of mother has been granted me, as that I have had laid upon me the task of carrying you around as a nurse! Yet just as the Lord once lovingly allowed Joseph to be his foster-father, and wanted him to be called 'father', so now he allows me too, your steward and servant, to be known as your
Cf. Bernard, Miss 2.16; SBOp 4:33-4; CF 18: 28-9. father or mother, by granting me that name.* Why should he do this, if it is not because these intimate names tell us of his own intimacy and because relationship in the spirit unites us no less than that of flesh and blood? But I have a witness and a partner in heaven
Cf. Job 16:20 when it comes to my love for you.* How I yearn, with maternal affection, to direct you to the heart of your true mother, who is

Christ. And just as it is right that I should feel this for all of you, so the same kind of affection binds you to me as to your parent, of whatever kind. Perhaps, as the apostle says, although I love you more, I am myself loved the less,* yet this too, fatherly love will pardon. As the same apostle says, parents ought to lay up treasure for the sons, not sons for parents!*

Cf. 2 Cor 12:15

Cf. 2 Cor 12:14

Let it be enough to have touched on this incidentally, in passing, though I hope the truths themselves will not pass!

8. Meanwhile, let us hasten back to the cross of Jesus with the blessed mother of the Lord and her companions, eager to measure the love of the crucified, as far as is right in view of our littleness. To stand there with greater strength and courage, let us, as the prophet says, 'stand there together.'* Let us draw one another by our mutual love to the contemplation of this immense love. I repeat, let us stand there together, and with hearts at one, let us marvel reverently at our prize and cleave to it wholly. Let our mouths be open wide to catch the liquid flowing gently from those wounds, more precious than fragrant balm, sweeter than honey. Let us swallow it with thirsting throat so that it may pour down into our heart and there search out every one of our ills, and in the searching, cure them. May that death live for us, may it be alive and breathe eternal life into our minds. His death lives eternally with his Father, it lives in the heavens, it lives in its purpose, it lives in its result. 'O death, I shall be your death,'* were the words of him who died on the cross for

Is 50:8

Hos 13:14

me. But this curse was for that death which devoured all our race.

9. But you, O death, which my Lord tasted through free choice not by force of circumstances and drained through love and not necessity, you are blessed and worthy to be blessed for all eternity. You commanded the great whale to spew us forth, or rather, you yourself gulped down our death to annihilate it utterly and wonderfully lodge us within yourself. The insatiable maw of that beast was ripped apart by your hook which it carelessly took and arrogantly swallowed,* and now all the prey, greedily crammed into its bowels for so many years past, is spilled forth. So you are alive from now into eternity, you are alive, you are triumphant, you are king. You live in the putting to death of sin, in the destruction of faults, you live in the tears of the contrite, the comfort of the sorrowful, the remitting of punishment. You live in the virtue of faith, in the devotion of the sacraments, above all in the minds and prayers of the loving. You live in the fidelity of the martyrs, you live in the life of the holy, and lastly and most blessedly, you live in their death.

Cf. Job 40:24

O death of my Lord, who could assess your priceless worth, by which you make the death of your saints also something precious?* You have made it possible for us not to flee from death, as from the sight of a snake, but instead, to flee towards it, running eagerly as to a mother's womb from which we shall soon be born anew as sons of life. Through your gracious mercy, we pass through death out

Cf. Ps 116:15

of death, into life, home to the fatherland. Let me say it again, you have made it possible for the death of the holy to be called rather an escape from death than a death, as the psalm says: 'And to the Lord, to the Lord, belongs the escape from death.'* For now that you have blessed it, the death of the saints is a coming safe to land from the vast sea of this long-lasting death, a restful anchorage, a harbor of peace, an entrance into joy. *Ps 68:20*

O victorious death, what is there still unconquered? Everywhere is bright with your triumphs, everywhere the banner of your victory flies in splendor. On our earth, you smashed the tombs and summoned from them the dead. From us, you sallied down to the underworld where you 'shattered the iron bars,'* where you pillaged its spoils, broke open its treasures and carried off with a masterful hand everything there that was precious. And then, you took your flight to the heavens, where you ceaselessly present yourself to the Father of mercies on behalf of the sin of the world, and you make reparation for it.* You alone, I repeat, can repay the debt of Adam and his sons to that eternal creditor. Therefore you are imperial on earth, irresistible in the underworld, glorious in the heavens. Here you inspire love, below you inspire terror, above you inspire veneration. *Ps 107:16* *Cf. Heb 7:15*

And this is how you marvelously enrich the left hand of the spouse, giving it magnificent splendor and making it supremely apt and 'rounded in a lathe' for the whole business of our salvation. A hand, as Solomon said,

Cf. Pr 10:4 rich indeed, and glorious,* which has been made precious by the standard of the cross, by the cleansing tide of blood, by the price of this most holy death. That hand has become the most secret and sacred treasury for all the weakness taken up by that majesty on our behalf.

10. Something had also to be said at this point about the right hand of the spouse and about the riches of salvation which it has prepared for us, but the length of this sermon demands that it be concluded. Tomorrow, by the grace of God, this debt will be paid, as far as he himself deigns to help us, for it is only through the generosity of his right hand that this and every good gift proceeds. May we be enabled worthily to praise and love the spouse of the church, Jesus Christ our Lord, who with the Father and the Holy Spirit lives and reigns, God, for ever and ever. Amen.

SERMON TWENTY-SEVEN

The beginning of the twenty-seventh sermon.
In praise of the right hand of the spouse, and of its fivefold glory, as if of the five fingers of his right hand.

'HIS HANDS ARE ROUNDING GOLD, filled with hyacinths.'* As far as my own ability goes, dearest brothers, I have no hope at all of being able to redeem the pledge I gave you yesterday, but he has a most generous right hand, which I am anxious to commend to your love. Oh, may it not be shortened in your regard by my attempt! May the Lord stretch down his hand from above, and for his good pleasure may he touch equally my lips and your heart! *Sg 5:14*

In my previous sermon I spoke of the left hand of the spouse, which is the weakness he took to himself for our sake, and how it was rounded on the lathe, by him and in him, in as many ways as there were different kinds of weakness to be experienced on our behalf. It was also not unfittingly called 'turned', because when that hand was rounded into the whole range of weakness by the universal craftsman, divine Wisdom,* it also turned, with a craftsman's skill, its supreme and amazing work of art, namely, our salvation. Look at the greatness of the skill and of the *Cf. Wis 7:22*

speed! Once 'he spoke, and everything was
Ps 33:9 made,'* then he suffered, and everything was made anew. So the word 'turned' is used of his hand, not only because it worked for us by suffering, but also because, saving us like this, it perfected its work. And let nobody be bold enough to ask me what this work of Jesus is. It is he himself you must ask, and his very name, Jesus, will give you the answer.

2. What else is the work of a savior but to save? Listen to the words of the prophet also. 'Yet our God is a king from of old, who does
Ps 74:12 saving deeds in the midst of the earth.'* And here is another saying: 'That he may work his
Is 28:21 work, his work is alien to himself.'* After all, what is more alien to saving power than to be weak? Nevertheless, to bring us salvation, the Wisdom of God, whose foresight controls all that is, cleverly fashioned this alien work into his own, that is, into a divine work. He worked on it with nimble artistry, and he brought it powerfully to a conclusion.

Consider also the zeal with which he applied himself to this work, and the charity with which he was on fire. 'My food', he said, 'is to do the will of my Father, that I
Jn 4:34 may perfect his work.'* Here you can see how hungry, or rather, how famished he was for our salvation. He was being fed every hour, because he was always working the will of his Father, and yet he never ceased to hunger until that work was perfected. I think it was this food the bride was meaning when she asked the spouse where he pastured at mid-
Cf. Sg 1:6 day.* Perhaps too, in that place where she said that the beloved was hers and she his,

and added, 'he pastures among the lilies.'* If I am not mistaken, her intention was to suggest that there had been a time when he pastured on food of this nature, but that 'at midday', he fed on something different. For it was then, namely, at the sixth hour, that he was crucified, and ate ashes as it were bread, and mingled his drink with his tears.* He was not pasturing then among the springtime beauty of the heavens, where lilies 'labor not, neither do they spin,'* but among the blood-stained thorns of his agony. Until he could eat no more, he was given as his food the punishment reserved for criminals, among whom he was numbered.* This was his food, then, and next he asked for a drink. He said, 'I thirst.'* It was as if he said, 'To the very last mouthful of death, all that meal has been finished. I took it from my Father's hand, and there I bring this supper to a close.' And therefore, when he had taken the vinegar, he said, 'It is finished,'* meaning that in that draught of vinegar he had tasted of death to the full. In that death, he proclaimed that the whole work of our salvation was finished, in so far as concerned the labor of the left hand.

Sg 2:16

Cf. Ps 102:9

Mt 6:28

Cf. Is 53:12

Jn 19:28

Jn 19:30

3. The time has come now for the left hand to rest from its labors and for the right hand to rise up and perfect the work of our salvation. For so we read in scripture: 'His right hand and his holy arm have brought him salvation.'* And again: 'The right hand of the Lord does valiantly, the right hand of the Lord lifted me up, the right hand of the Lord does valiantly.'* 'Awake, then, awake,

Ps 98:1

Ps 118:16

put on strength, right arm of the Lord!
Is 51:9 Awake,' he says, 'as in days of old!'* You will have noticed, I am sure, how the glory of this right arm is praised by David in three different ways, and that likewise it is by a threefold appeal that Isaiah calls or rather challenges it to arise. Three times also that same right hand is glorified in the canticle of Moses, when he cries aloud in joyful song: 'Your right hand, O Lord, glorious in power, your right hand, O Lord, shatters the enemy, and in the greatness of your glory you have
Ex 15:6,7 laid low those who attack me.'*

To take a shortcut, let us look more closely at this threefold enumeration of glory: 'The right hand of the Lord does valiantly,' raising Christ to life from the dead; 'the right hand of the Lord lifted me up,' lifting Christ up above all the heavens; 'the right hand of the Lord does valiantly', glorifying Christ in the faith of all the nations by sending the Paraclete. There is still one glorification of Christ lacking here, though it is as great as all the rest, and that is when he will come in his glory, and the glory of his Father and his holy angels, to transform the body of our lowliness
Cf. Ph 3:21 into the body of his splendor.* Then at last he will have put the finishing touch to the work of our salvation.

These are the four titles Christ has to glory, but before them, chief among them and greater than all, in fact the basis of them all, is the great condescension of the Word, beyond any human power to describe or imagine. By it he united that man to himself, with the utmost graciousness and irresistible strength. When the Son called on his Father concerning this glory, with the words, 'Father, glorify your son', he received the reply, 'I have glorified him and I shall glorify him again.'* And again, when Christ was explaining at length to the crowd about his sheep, and promising to give them everlasting life, he finished his sermon with these words: 'What my Father has given to me is greater than all these things, and no one is able to snatch it out of my Father's hand. The Father and I are one.'*

Jn 12:28

Jn 10:29

Therefore the right hand of the spouse is the glory of Jesus Christ. 'He was predestinated Son of God in power,'* and it was glory indeed that he received from his Father's hand in time, because of his holy union with the divine Word.

Rom 1:4

4. Consequently, as we have said, there is a fivefold division of glory here, so that, as is fitting, his right hand may have five fingers. The first is that the man Christ was taken up into a glorious union with the Word of God, and this may be called the thumb of his right hand, being more powerful than all the other fingers by virtue of its strength and dignity. The second is that, like the sun at morning, he burst forth on the third day from the sepulchre, though it was guarded with a stone and seals and a detachment of soldiers. He brought the glory of his resurrection to all who would believe in him, and he changed the three days' sorrow of his new bride into swift and everlasting joy. For it was impossible for the man who was glorified in God to be a prisoner of death for more than

three days, as he himself prophesied to his bride. Speaking of the speedy glorification of the son of man, he said of himself, 'If God is glorified in him, then God will glorify him in
Jn 13:32 himself, and swiftly will he glorify him.'* As if to say, 'My little children, do not be afraid. You are mourning over my approaching death, but in a little while you shall see me in my glory. For there cannot be any delay in the glory of resurrection for the man whom the only Son of God has already taken up into his own glory.'

The third finger of the right hand is that he is exalted in the splendor of the heavens, lifted up into the glory of the Father and established on the Father's throne of glory. All things, whether in heaven or earth, are
Cf. Ps 8:6 under his feet.* The fourth is that he distributes the gifts of grace according to his will. After Pentecost he poured out the Holy Spirit without restraint on all the earth, that he might glorify his name, and now today, according to the measure of his giving, as
Cf. Eph 4:7 scripture says,* he does not hesitate to give out those same waters in his fist. The fifth is that every eye will see him on the glorious throne of his majesty, when time has come to an end, All the more for being so long hidden, his glory will shine forth in splendor beyond all the astonished mind can conceive.

Hence this fivefold glory of the spouse is referred to as 'turned by the lathe' by the bride, because, as we have already frequently pointed out, it is devised with fine artistry and carried out with the utmost speed.

5. Are you eager to understand craft and

craftsman in one short word? 'The Word was made flesh.'* Take note how speedy the art is in consequence. At the very same hour, at the very same moment, the divine greatness stooped low and humanity was raised aloft, and when the Only Son of God became the son of man, the son of man became likewise in all reality the Only Son of God. But it was the divine greatness alone that achieved this glorification of the son of man, covering him, as scripture says, 'with blessings of sweetness.'* Then in all that followed, that man, who had been marvelously taken up into the Word of God, wonderfully and magnificently worked in partnership with him, as we read: 'Awake, awake, put on strength, right arm of the Lord!'* 'Awake', it says, 'awake', that is, 'work in partnership with your Father in the work of your glorification.' In short, the Father raised him from the dead, glorifying his Son, and yet nevertheless, he raised himself from the dead, according to his own words, 'I have power to lay down my life and I have power to take it up again.'* Likewise, 'I shall lift up my hand to heaven,'* says the Father, while it is to the Son of God that it is said, 'Be lifted up, Lord, in your power!'* In the name of the Son, the Father sent the Holy Spirit, and then that same Son says of himself, 'If I go away, I shall send him to you.'* With reference, too, to the power of judgement, it is said, 'He has given him the authority to execute judgement, because he is the son of man.'* While scripture says of the son of man, 'it is he who has set up his throne of judgement.'*

Jn 1:14
Cf. Ps 21:3
Is 51:9
Jn 10:18
Deut 32:40
Ps 21:13
Jn 16:7
Jn 5:27
Ps 9:7

So the right hand of the spouse is this fivefold glory of Jesus Christ, and, as said before, it is called 'turned' because it is carried out by the Wisdom of God with a craftsman's speed.

6. There is this reason, too, why the right hand may quite fittingly be described as 'turning', and that is the sheer skill with which it prepared the work of our salvation. The left hand, as was shown above, saved us in weakness, but 'the salvation of the right
Ps 20:6 hand' is 'in might'.* Take careful note, brothers, of the extraordinary speed and sureness of this lathe-work. In every single one of the deeds that brought him glory, that right hand was mightily engaged in every single one of the concerns that would bring us glory, too. By grace of the Word, as soon as the fruit of the virgin's womb was taken up into the indescribable nature of the Word, at the same instant, we were also completely lifted above ourselves and with miraculous mercy given a share in this glory. Through the power of the same grace, the son of man was made God and we, sons of Adam, sons of a sinner, were made sons of God, by reason of our faith in Christ.

Christ, of course, inherited that title to glory in a manner far more sublime. In his case there is the mystery of that most sacred union that makes him Son, but in a manner that also makes him, the only Son. With us, however, it is very different. We are sons in the sense of being adopted by the Father through his only Son, yet, thanks to that everlasting and astonishing love, pouring out the riches of his oil on the man of his right hand,* he poured out on us, too, the unction of his riches. Let the blessed prerogative of his name be kept for the Lord our God, while on my part, I fully admit, and rejoice in it, that my glory is nothing but a sharing in his. In short, I can be convinced that it is this that supremely glorifies me, because 'he who comes from heaven is above all',* and none among the sons of God either is or can be like the Only-begotten.

Cf. Ps 121:5

Jn 3:32

Yet however great the Son of God is, he is all mine! At his very conception the Father laid upon him glory and great beauty, beyond all thought or understanding,* but the Father has given him to me, and has he not bestowed with him all that is his?* The crown of glory set upon his head belongs now to this head of mine, and does that not give me a right to take pride in it?

Cf. Ps 21:5

Cf. Rom 8:32

7. In the same way, I have a right to claim for myself no small share in the glory of the resurrection. My Lord triumphed over the sting of death for this precise reason, that he himself might become the cause whereby all who are united to him triumph over death. Now if his death was so strong and life-giving as to utterly vanquish death, swing open the prisons of the dead and summon them to come forth, is it not more likely that the full riches of this glory will belong to the resurrection? He is by right 'first-born among the dead',* for only he was 'free among the dead',* but I have a share in that freedom, and except for the first fruits of salvation which are his by right as the first-born, as

Cf. Col 1:18

Cf. Ps 88:4

I have a share in his freedom, so with unshakable faith I hope to have a share in his resurrection.

Deeply incised on the tablets of my heart, inviolably reposing within my breast, is the most certain hope that my Redeemer has come back to life in order that with and in him I too may live again.* *Cf. Job 19:27* Mounting up then into the heavens, he drew my eyes there after him, and he 'hung up my soul.'* *Cf. Job 7:15* My eyes and my soul will not faint, until he shows himself to me and, through his grace, makes me in turn present to him. But oh, better to say, if only my soul would faint, and my eyes also, faint into Jesus, until both become glorious with the blessed revelation of his glory! But meantime, while this life lasts, I abandon myself with the total freedom of hope to the deeply held conviction of the apostle, who proclaimed that we sit together with Christ in the heavenly places.* *Cf. Eph 2:6* Our lofty eagle spread wide his pinions, and winged his way to the heavens with his eaglets.

8. Therefore, we are saved, here and now, as regards the virtue of hope, and salvation is already perfected, as regards its cause and mystery. 'His right hand,' he says, brought him salvation, 'and his holy arm.'* *Ps 98:1* It brought him salvation, because in establishing a most perfect and powerful cause of salvation he indeed accomplished his work, but the effect of the salvation has not yet flowed out to us in its fulness. Therefore, it was to him that it 'brought salvation', while for us, from now until the end of time, it never rests from offering to save.

In the bestowal of gifts and the gift of the Paraclete, which is the outstanding glory of the riches of the Lord Jesus, the great share of my glory, as one of his humble members, is this, to share according to the measure of his generosity and my capacity, one of the hyacinths with which his right hand is full. Whatever is lacking in the share I have of glory, it is most richly made up to me in the rich fullness of his glory, to my unbounded joy and delight.

Finally, we await with certain hope for the total glory of the spouse to be most blessedly consummated. Then all the glory we have spoken of above will be openly revealed, both in the king of glory himself and in the vessels of his glory, which we ourselves are. The splendor of that day of his, most magnificent, great and various, will shine out for his saints with infinitely beautiful brightness, will flash out for the wicked with infinitely terrible bolts of lightning.

On that day we expect to see both hands of the spouse come to the perfect end of their lathe-work. Before time began, he devised that work in company with his Father, and from the beginning of time right up to the very last day, he never wearies from laboring at it with tireless solicitude, with indefatigable love, with the most delicate care and wisdom. It is an extraordinary work, and for all eternity, as is right and just, it will be praised. All will cry out together in one great hymn that never ends: 'Salvation to our God, who sits upon the throne, and to the Lamb!'* May we be granted to enter into *Rev 7:10*

the praise of the glory of him to whom salvation belongs and who alone is worthy to be eternally hymned! May he grant us this,
Cf. Ps 68:20 'the God of our salvation',*
Jesus Christ our Lord, who
with God the Father and
the Holy Spirit, lives
and reigns, God,
for ever and
ever.
Amen.

SERMON TWENTY-EIGHT

The beginning of the twenty-eighth sermon. How the 'belly' of the spouse indicates his mercy, yet in as much as it is 'a block of ivory', it represents justice, the inseparable companion of mercy. The studding with sapphires is the tranquility of those who gaze upon the merciful justice and just mercy of God.

'HIS BELLY A BLOCK OF IVORY, studded with sapphires.'* The loving *Sg 5:14* words of this song have a mysterious sweetness that ravishes the hearts of lovers with delight. Yet the more closely the eyes are fixed upon their depths, the more terrible their profundity appears. The more profound the depths, however, the richer the whole content of meaning and the more poignant the delight. And in the entire length of this marriage hymn, I do not know if any words can be found more obscure than these, in which the bride, as is her due, pours out her whole soul in praise of her beloved. It is easy to see that it is not she that speaks, but the Spirit of her Father who speaks within her.* For wherever he is, he glorifies Jesus, *Cf. Mt 10:20* as the Lord himself promised when he said, 'He will glorify me, for he will take what is mine and declare it to you.'* And again, *Jn 16:14* 'When the Paraclete comes, whom I shall send

you from the Father, he will bear witness to
Jn 15:26 me.'* It is hardly to be wondered at if the Spirit of truth should wholly abandon himself to the praise of one seeing that, from the very first moment of his conception, he poured himself out, to anoint him. If only in our hearts, too, that Spirit would bear witness to the Truth, whose Spirit he is! Then, 'from a
1 Tim 1:5 pure heart and a good conscience,'* we too might be found worthy to witness to the Truth, to search into the solemn words of Jesus and proclaim their meaning.

2. So, from the 'rounding hands' of the spouse, in which we hold that Christ's voluntary weakness and his glorified humanity are being commended by the Holy Spirit, the song of praise progresses logically enough to his power of judging. The emphasis laid on this power of his will be, as it were, by way of recompense for the weakness he took upon himself, and a glorious fulfillment of his glorification. But to praise this strength is frightening, and could be too overwhelming for the maidens of Jerusalem. So the bride couples mercy with justice, or rather, justice with mercy, that is, delicately commending one after the other, and one by the other, using the symbol of 'the ivory belly'.

For the prophet, 'belly' signified loving mercy, as when he says, 'My belly moans like
Is 16:11 a lyre for Moab.'* In case someone finds this obscure, he added, 'And my heart for Kirhareseth.'* Another prophet, too, speaks in the same sense, 'I suffer in my heart, I suffer in
Jer 4:19 my heart!'* I think you also have noticed the explanation for this meaning of the word.

It is sufficiently obvious that within the belly is the source of emotion. And we cannot but know the heart of our God in all its tender mercy; it is something we must never forget, it is how the 'dayspring from on high' came to us and comes to us still.* *Cf. Lk 1:78* How great that heart, how wide, how incomprehensible! In the nature of things, what can be imagined as being more loving than the heart of a father or mother? But such are the riches of God's heart that he has bound us to himself by a double cord of love, both as a father, shaping us into his own image and likeness,* *Cf. Gen 1:26* and as a mother carrying us within the womb and bringing us to birth, even at the cost of suffering.

If I compare my father and mother to the divine mercy, there is a sense in which they are not so much parents as parricides! For it was they who first flung forth into this mortal life one conceived and brought to birth in sin, and destined in the end to be enwrapped in unending darkness. But the Lord, my God, holds within himself the love of both parents, and he brought me forth in holiness and immortality. Listen to a mother yearning over her children: 'Can a mother forget her child, and not take pity on the son of her womb? And even if she should forget, yet shall I not forget you.'* *Is 49:15* And again: 'As a mother cherishes her children, so shall I cherish you.'* *Is 66:13* And once again: 'I was like a nurse to Ephraim, and they did not know that it was I who looked after them.'* *Hos 11:3*

3. But now let us come to the very words of Incarnate Wisdom, words sweeter even

than honey. His passion was close at hand,
and he was on the point of going down into
that vast ocean of his suffering, in which
Pharaoh with all his chariots and horsemen
Cf. Ex 15:4 had to be drowned.* He comforted his little
ones with words so tender, he gave them such
gentle teaching about love, he encouraged
them with such gracious promises of soon
sending the Holy Spirit, that he might well be
considered as having then opened the flood-
gates of his heart. When he had finished
speaking, he turned away from them for a
Cf. Lk 22:41 while, the evangelist tells us,* to pray to his
Father for them, with greater privacy and
earnestness. 'Turned away' is the right ex-
pression to use. At that time he was com-
pletely overcome with maternal love,
enduring in his breast indescribable pangs
of an utterly overwhelming affection, at
having to abandon them like orphans and be
'turned away' from those for whose sake he
did not hesitate to die. So he offered his
heart to his Father and 'being in an agony,' as
the evangelist says, 'his sweat became as drops
Lk 22:43,44 of blood, trickling down upon the earth.'*
Perhaps someone thinks it was dread of his
approaching passion that aroused that
anguish in the heart of Jesus and wrung a
bloody sweat from his body. But both were
caused, not by fear, but by loving mercy.

As the hour of his passion drew near, the
gospels tell us that Jesus began to be weary,
Cf. Mk 14:33 distressed and troubled,* but that was no
more than the beginning. Suffering of that
kind he underwent of his own free will, he
controlled it by his own power, and he threw

it off when he pleased. It was through love he accepted it, not through necessity, through tender compassion, not slavish fate. If you would understand the deeper reasons for this agony and sweat, there is one who lay on the breast of Jesus and entered into a knowledge of this mystery: ask him.* He had the privilege both to witness and relate all that Jesus said in that lengthy prayer which breathed out solely love and tender mercy. All who would reverently understand that most sacred mercy will be able to see in those words, with the utmost clarity, what a struggle there was in the depths of the tender heart of Jesus, what tortures of compassion, what a battle of merciful tenderness, what agonies of love. Hence those words in the psalm, 'My heart has become like wax, melting within my belly.'* The heart of Jesus is his love, but his belly is his mercy.

Cf. Jn 13:23

Ps 22:14

Often enough, love does not appear as melting, or as fleshly or waxen, but seems rather to be like hard bone or a rock—for example, when love teaches, exhorts, accuses, strikes, beats. Indeed, up to this hour, this was the kind of love the Lord Jesus showed his disciples, but now was the very moment when he must be 'turned away' from them, and he could control his heart no longer. His heart became 'within his belly like melting wax',* because love turned all to gentleness from the intimate depths of tender mercy. O loving Jesus! how merciful, how concerned, how rich in compassion the desire of that heart as it prayed that the Father might keep them in his name, sanctifying them in truth, unite

Ibid.

them in love, join them to their head and make them happy in the vision of that glory
Cf. Jn 17:11 which the Father had given him. This love of the heart of Jesus, though at that time, expressed and offered amongst the little flock
Cf. Lk 12:32 which the Father had given to him, was not wholly poured out upon it.

4. But it would be more true to say that his love has been unreservedly poured out on them, and yet it has still, nevertheless, to be poured out on all the others as well. For 'his name is as oil poured out,' and therefore the
Cf. Sg 1:2 maidens love him exceedingly,* those of lesser merit too, and not only she whose superabundant charity has won her the name and the honor of bride. That out-poured oil has drenched the lesser maidens also. The Spirit of Jesus is like the soul of his whole body, so totally diffused throughout each separate part that one life animates all, totally present in the whole and in each individual member. And so we, who now appear on the scene after so many centuries, we too are held within that belly of infinite tenderness, and indeed, through his mercy, were held within it even then. For in days gone by, not the least glory in the adornment of the high priest was to have inscribed on his
Cf. Ex 39:14 breast the names of all the tribes of Israel;* but the glory of Jesus is greater. When Jesus was about to go in to the altar of God, that is, to the altar of incense, to his charity, when he was about to offer himself in sacrifice to his Father for the sake of us all, a breastplate clung to his body, far more glorious and holy. On that breastplate, he held out to his Father

in humble entreaty the names not only of all the tribes of Israel, but of every single son of Israel, that is, not just the apostles, but all those also who through their word would come to believe in him.* *Cf. Jn 17:20*

The charity of Christ was poured out into the heart of Paul* to such a degree that each weakness and fall of each individual weakened him and burned him up,* and the pressure of charity forced him to cry out, now for this reason and now for that, 'I suffer in my heart, I suffer in my heart!'* How much more, then, the belly of Christ, hardly able to contain a heart so great, stretches out into an immense infinity from the overflowing richness of tender mercy? For if the streams of living water pour with such abundance from the belly of Paul, or of any other of those who love him,* how much more must the belly of Christ be an abyss of tender mercy, wholly deep and unfathomable? *Cf. Rom 5:5* *Cf. 2 Cor 11:29* *Jer 4:19* *Cf. Jn 7:38*

5. We must admit that indeed 'he bore our sorrows,' then, all of them, 'and carried our griefs,'* by sharing fully in what we suffer, too, today. If even then he pleaded with the Father on account of the sins which he foresaw I would one day commit, and for them he offered his soul in sacrifice, so his tender mercy suffered, truly with my sorrows and weaknesses, the very ones that even today he is ever anxious to heal with his overflowing goodness. *Is 53:4*

It was then, as I have said, that the fountain of all tender mercy, the 'ivory belly' of the Lord Jesus, streamed out to form springs and rivers. Before Pilate condemned him to mount

the cross that was waiting, he had already experienced a far more bitter cross in the emotional tumult of love that was tearing him apart. Who would venture to expound the depths of the grief to which he had freely abandoned himself when he said, 'My soul is
Mt 26:38 sorrowful to the point of death?'* Truly,
Cf. Lam 1:12 there is no sorrow like that sorrow,* that bears the weight of all sorrows. He saw in advance how his bride would meet disaster, the countless shocks and the intense persecution, even to the end of time. He knew the many trials and evils, and just as he saw them in advance, so likewise he experienced them in advance, in his compassion. The emotion of love bore fiercely down upon the winepress of tender pity, and wrung out from the heart and body of the Lord Jesus those drops of bloody sweat. And so, in that agony, as in everything else, Love triumphed over Jesus.

I put my trust in the inexhaustibly tender mercy of my Lord, as much now as in the past. Although on the cross he was exposed to such heat that his strength 'dried up like a
Cf. Ps 22:15 potsherd',* and all the anguish of his distress poured out from him in a sweat of blood, nevertheless, he is my head and I am a part of his body, however small. So I can never know any wound or bruise or grief which he does not suffer with me, which he, in a word, does not heal. Such is the very close partnership, the covenant, the union, the kiss of peace between us, though the head may shine out resplendent in glory and the body, in this present life, seem mean and lowly.

So 'the belly of the spouse' is the tenderness

and richness of his compassion, which he lavishes upon his bride in countless ways in all her countless needs.

6. But what is the point of calling this belly 'a block of ivory', since ivory is wholly without a capacity for tenderness? Its coldness seems hardly in accord with the longing of the bride as she throws her arms about it. In my opinion, then, as I recall having said before, as well as gentle mercy, the Holy Spirit is pointing out the spouse's justice. It seems to me not unfitting that zeal for justice should be indicated by means of ivory teeth, and of course I have been persuaded to this belief by reading that Solomon built himself a stately throne of ivory.* This obviously represents Christ's judgement-seat. Moreover, he coated it completely with a sheathe of gleaming gold, to indicate that even in judgement, mercy is to be exalted upon judgement. What Solomon symbolized by ivory covered with gold is here symbolized also, by the ivory belly, and again it is Solomon, the true 'Solomon', Christ our 'peacemaker'.* In one case the ivory throne, sheathed in gold, is said to be justice adorned with tender mercy; in the other case, the ivory belly is tender mercy encompassed with justice. One is merciful justice, the other just mercy.

Cf. 1 Kgs 10:18

A reference to the meaning of 'Solomon'.

Jacob said something similar when he was about to be laid with his fathers, and lifted up his eyes to his Lord and son. 'His eyes are more beautiful than wine,' he said, 'and his teeth are whiter than milk.'* What was he trying to say by 'teeth whiter than milk'? Surely what David meant when he said,

Gen 49:12

'Your judgements are sweet, more desirable
Ps 19:10 than gold, than much precious metal.'* So there is the same meaning, because there is the same Spirit, and gilt and ivory teeth establish our Solomon–Christ on a throne, while teeth whiter than milk beautify his mouth. This is because mercy and truth go
Cf. Ps 89:14 before him to prepare his throne,* or rather, they meet him on the very throne itself. For we find it written, 'In merciful love will his
Is 16:5 royal seat be established.'* And again, 'He has
Hos 9:8 established his throne in justice.'* So let us
Cf. Heb 4:16 come near to that throne, wholly confident* that, 'however angry he has been, he will
Hab 3:2 always remember his mercy.'*

When we come to him on the day of judgement, his belly, block of ivory though it may be, will not repress his compassionate love. God will not forget to show pity, even in that solemn setting. It will be then, in fact, that there is the greatest need to show pity and the very last hour for his mercy. Or rather, that hour will make it absolutely clear what a heart of tenderest mercy his ivory belly contains, its greatness, its nature, its responsiveness. On that day all the vessels of mercy will be filled to overflowing with his tender compassion.

7. The 'studding with sapphires' seems to me to indicate quite plainly the different rewards God will give us. The Jerusalem which is above, whose ruins we shall see built up into wholeness on that judgement day, was solemnly promised, 'I shall lay your foundations in sapphires.'* And when Ezekiel saw
Is 54:11
the glorious throne of the God of Israel, it

had the appearance of a sapphire.* Consequently, the sapphire, which resembles the tranquil heavens, represents the tranquility of the souls that gaze upon the countenance of glory, never ceasing, never knowing repletion, never feeling weary. It is upon stones like this, four-square, that our mother is built, that glorious city of Zion,* although she is to be far more renowned and wonderful through her being studded so intricately with sapphires. This is the reason why his belly will appear as a block of ivory studded with sapphires, so that from that very studding, the last day will make unmistakably evident that God's mercy comes in many shapes, his wisdom likewise.

Cf. Ez 1:26

Cf. Is 28:16

To the splendor of that blessed vision may we, too, be led, together with his bride, by the only Son of the Father, the spouse of the church, Jesus Christ our Lord, who with the same Father and the Holy Spirit lives and reigns, God, for ever and ever. Amen.

CISTERCIAN PUBLICATIONS INC.

TITLES LISTING

THE CISTERCIAN FATHERS SERIES

THE CISTERCIAN STUDIES SERIES

* *Temporarily out of print* † *Forthcoming*

Symeon the New Theologian. Theological and Practical Treatises and Three Theological Discourses . . . CS 41†

Guigo II the Carthusian. The Ladder of Monks and Twelve Meditations . CS48

The Monastic Rule of Iosif Volotsky . . . . CS 36

CHRISTIAN SPIRITUALITY

The Spirituality of Western Christendom . . . . CS 30

Russian Mystics (Sergius Bolshakoff) CS 26

In Quest of the Absolute: The Life and Works of Jules Monchanin (J. G. Weber) . . . . CS 51

The Name of Jesus (Irenée Hausherr) . . . . CS 44

Entirely for God: A Life of Cyprian Tansi (Elizabeth Isichei) . . . . CS 43

Abba: Guides to Wholeness and Holiness East and West . . . . CS 38

MONASTIC STUDIES

The Abbot in Monastic Tradition (Pierre Salmon) . . . . CS 14

Why Monks? (François Vandenbroucke) . . . . CS 17

Silence in the Rule of St Benedict (Ambrose Wathen) . . . . CS 22

One Yet Two: Monastic Tradition East and West . . . . CS 29

Community and Abbot in the Rule of St Benedict I (Adalbert de Vogüé) . CS 5/1

Consider Your Call: A Theology of the Monastic Life (Daniel Rees et al) . CS 20

Households of God (David Parry) . . CS 39

CISTERCIAN STUDIES

The Cistercian Spirit (M. Basil Pennington, ed.) . . . . . . CS 3

The Eleventh-Century Background of Cîteaux (Bede K. Lackner) . . . . . . CS 8

Contemplative Community . . . . CS 21

Cistercian Sign Language (Robert Barakat) . . . . CS 11

The Cistercians in Denmark (Brian P. McGuire) . . . . CS 35

Saint Bernard of Clairvaux: Essays Commemorating the Eighth Centenary of His Canonization . . CS 28

Bernard of Clairvaux: Studies Presented to Dom Jean Leclercq . . . . CS 23

Bernard of Clairvaux and the Cistercian Spirit (Jean Leclercq) . . . . CS 16

William of St Thierry: The Man and His Work (J. M. Déchanet) . . . . CS 10

Aelred of Rievaulx: A Study (Aelred Squire) . . . . CS 50

Christ the Way: The Christology of Guerric of Igny (John Morson) . . CS 25

The Golden Chain: The Theological Anthropology of Isaac of Stella (Bernard McGinn) . . . . CS 15

Studies in Cistercian Art and Architecture, I (Meredith Lillich, ed) . . CS 66

Studies in Medieval Cistercian History sub-series

Studies I . . . . CS 13

Studies II . . . . CS 24

Cistercian Ideals and Reality (Studies III) . . . . CS 60

Simplicity and Ordinariness (Studies IV) . . . . CS 61

The Chimera of His Age: Studies on St Bernard (Studies V) . . . . CS 63

Cistercians in the Late Middle Ages (Studies VI) . . . . CS 64

Noble Piety and Reformed Monasticism (Studies VII) . . . . CS 65

Benedictus: Studies in Honor of St Benedict of Nursia (Studies VIII) . CS 67

Heaven on Earth (Studies IX) . . . . CS 68†

THOMAS MERTON

The Climate of Monastic Prayer . . . . CS 1

Thomas Merton on St Bernard . . . . . CS 9

Thomas Merton's Shared Contemplation: A Protestant Perspective (Daniel J. Adams) . . . . CS 62

Solitude in the Writings of Thomas Merton (Richard Anthony Cashen) . . . . . CS 40

The Message of Thomas Merton (Brother Patrick Hart, ed.) . . . . . CS 42

FAIRACRES PRESS, OXFORD

The Wisdom of the Desert Fathers

The Letters of St Antony the Great

The Letters of Ammonas, Successor of St Antony

A Study of Wisdom. Three Tracts by the author of *The Cloud of Unknowing*

The Power of the Name. The Jesus Prayer in Orthodox Spirituality (Kallistos Ware)

Solitude and Communion

Contemporary Monasticism

A Pilgrim's Book of Prayers (Gilbert Shaw)

Theology and Spirituality (Andrew Louth)

** Temporarily out of print* *† Forthcoming*